Old Wine
In New Skins

Calls To Worship
And Other Worship Resources

George A. Nye

CSS Publishing Company, Inc.
Lima, Ohio

Scripture quotations are from:
The *Holy Bible, New International Version.* Copyright (c) 1973, 1978, 1984 International Bible Society. Used by permission of Zondervan Bible Publishers. All rights reserved.

The *Revised Standard Version of the Bible,* copyrighted 1946, 1952, (c), 1971, 1973, by the Division of Christian Education of the National Council of the Churches of Christ in the USA. Used by permission.

And the *New Revised Standard Version of the Bible,* copyright 1989 by the Division of Christian Education of the National Council of the Churches of Christ in the USA. Used by permission.

Library of Congress Cataloging-in-Publication Data

Nye, George A., 1937-
Old wine in new skins : calls to worship and other worship resources / by George A. Nye.
p.   cm.
ISBN 1-55673-824-2
1. Worship programs. 2. Gathering rites. I. Title.
BV198.N94   1994
254—dc20   93-38001
                                                                CIP

ISBN 1-55673-824-2   PRINTED IN U.S.A.

To my beloved
life's companion
Sandra McCrory Nye

Table Of Contents

Introduction

I have lived with the tension of seeking to maintain traditional forms of the worship service, on the one hand, and responding to the newer features of worship that have become so popular in recent years, on the other. The worship aids which are featured in this book are a mixture of traditional and contemporary responses, many of which intersperse congregational singing in the call to worship. Some of the hymns are steeped in the tradition of the church and others are lively contemporary songs that lift our emotions up to the throne of grace.

Hymns that belong to the public domain and no longer require copyright acknowledgment, are printed into the text. The hymns and songs that do require copyright permission are listed in the text by title and tune or author, with the suggestions of what verses to use, at which spot. If you have already secured your Christian Copyright Licensing International number, you are encouraged to copy the words into your bulletin for use in your local worship service. This saves switching back and forth from hymnal to bulletin, and makes a much better flow of dialogue and music. By paying your annual fee to this organization, you may ethically and legally copy the words of the songs into your bulletin for use in your church. If you have not secured your copyright license, you may do so by contacting: Christian Copyright Licensing International, 6130 N.E. 78th Court, Suite C-11, Portland, Oregon 97218.

Nearly all hymns and songs used in this book may be found in *Hymns For The Family Of God,* Paragon Press, and *Maranatha! Music: Praise & Worship Collection.*

In the section on calls to worship that include personal preparation, I have given some examples of how to prepare people for worship without a formal responsive reading. I hope this stretches your imagination to branch out in other areas of reflection, as worship begins. You might use different biblical characters who were confronted by God, briefly examine their stories, and then relate them to the people in the congregation. How would they respond? Are they as prepared or unprepared, are they as faithful or unbelieving as the biblical person, to God's approach?

Possibilities for different Sundays include Sarai, cackling with laughter when God's representative says that she'll become pregnant; Jacob receiving a blessing from God that disables him in the process; Jesus accepting Peter's challenge in the midst of the stormy sea and Peter's lack of faith when he acts upon Jesus' gift; the Samaritan woman being pushed and repeatedly brought back on track until she becomes honest with herself and with Jesus, so that he can redeem her; Zacchaeus, hoping for a glimpse of the Master, finding himself hosting Jesus at dinner, and then discovering what salvation costs.

In each case, the congregation can be challenged to identify with the biblical person, as the individuals present search their own lives for the answers: "Am I prepared to receive more of Jesus than I anticipated when I came to church today?" "Am I prepared to get honest with myself, and with the Lord, and find my life radically changed and reformed, as a result?" "Am I ready to risk the probability that Jesus will act upon my petition, which will require a response of faith from me?" Then move into a reflective prayer of preparation before introducing the opening hymn.

The materials in the "Preparation For Pastoral Prayer" grew out of my frustration that we limit ourselves too severely compared to what is available to us through prayer. In worship, or in a Wednesday evening service, when I ask for prayer concerns, the response invariably centers on tumors and broken bones. Those calamities are worthy of prayer, but there is so much more to prayer than praying just for physical disease and trauma that I started developing prayer themes in the worship service. Sometimes the mood is set by a medley of songs that develop a theme. Often it is set by a devotional reflection which I give at the beginning of our prayer time. The purpose is two-fold: to accomplish the experience of prayerful communication with God and to help people broaden their understanding of the many ways that we can approach the Lord in prayer.

May the Lord bless you as you regularly seek to lift the people up in worship and praise of our majestic God.

1 — Calls To Worship With Praise And Celebration

Number 1

Pastor: O Lord, our Lord,

People: O Lord, our Lord, how majestic is your name in all the earth!

Pastor: You have set your glory

People: You have set your glory above the heavens.

Pastor: From the lips of children

People: From the lips of children you have ordained praise.

Pastor: When I consider your heavens,

People: And the work of your fingers,

Pastor: What is a human being that you are mindful of him,

People: And the child of humanity, that you care for her?

Pastor: And yet,

People: And yet, you made him a little less than God.

Pastor: And crowned her with glory and honor.

People: What can we do but praise?

Pastor: What can we do but worship?

People: O Lord, our Lord, how majestic is your name in all the earth! *(Based on Psalm 8)*

Praise Hymn: "O Lord, Our Lord How Majestic Is Your Name" Michael W. Smith

Invocation and Lord's Prayer

Number 2

Pastor: "For God so loved the world,"

People: "Surely"

Pastor: "That he gave his only begotten son,"

People: "Surely goodness and mercy"

Pastor: "That whoever believes in him,"

People: "Surely goodness and mercy shall follow me,"

Pastor: "Should not perish but have eternal life."

People: Surely goodness and mercy shall follow me all the days of my life."

Pastor: "For God sent the Son into the world,"

People: "And I,"

Pastor: "Not to condemn the world,"

People: "And I shall dwell,"

Pastor: "But that the world, through him, might be saved."

People: "And I shall dwell in the house of the Lord"

Pastor: "Truly I say to you, he who hears my word and believes in him who sent me, has eternal life, and does not come into judgment, but has passed from death to life."

People: "And I shall dwell in the house of the Lord forever."
(John 3:16-17, 5:24, Psalm 23:6 RSV)

Hymn "Jesus Saves"

Alternate Hymn: "Rejoice, The Lord Is King" Darwall's 148th

Invocation and Lord's Prayer

Number 3

Pastor: "Happy are those whose way is blameless, who walk in the law of the Lord!"

People: "Happy are those who keep his testimonies, who seek him with their whole heart,"

Pastor: "Who also do no wrong,"

People: "But walk in his ways." *(Psalm 119:1-3 RSV)*

Pastor: These are beautiful words.

People: About whom are they speaking? Certainly not about us.

Pastor: They are words that describe the people of God.

People: We are the people of God. But we don't always seek him with our "whole hearts," and we cannot say that we walk in ways that are "blameless." We are among those who have sinned and fallen short of the glory of God.

Pastor: But with the apostle Paul, we are able to say, "Thanks be to God through Jesus Christ our Lord! ... There is therefore, now, no condemnation for those who are in Christ Jesus." *(Romans 7:25, 8:1 NRSV)*

People: Then in worship we shall come before God, with praises on our lips. For we are justified in Christ our Lord. "All hail the power of Jesus' name!"

Hymn: "All Hail The Power of Jesus' Name"

Invocation and Lord's Prayer

Number 4

Pastor: Immortal God!

People: From everlasting to everlasting, you are the same.

Pastor: Invisible Lord!

People: In my heart, in my home, in our world, in your universe, you are ever present.

Pastor: God only wise.

People: You are the fount of all knowledge, the source of all wisdom, the one who plants within our brains the ability to learn and the capacity to understand.

Pastor: Almighty One, victorious One, your great name we praise!

People: For your name encompasses that which is holy and gracious and defines the boundaries of goodness.

Pastor: Great Father of glory,

People: We dare to claim the exalted title: children of God.

Pastor: Pure Father of light,

People: We come before you with our lives open to your searching light of truth.

Pastor: Your angels adore you.

People: With thanksgiving on our lips, we proclaim our affection for you.

Pastor: We stand in your splendor,

People: That your majesty might enfold us with your redeeming love.

Hymn: "Immortal, Invisible, God Only Wise" (St. Denio)

Invocation and Lord's Prayer

Number 5

Pastor: I feel like singing this morning, O Lord.

People: We have a song in our hearts that is yearning to get out.

Pastor: I feel like telling everyone around me how great you are.

People: There rests in our souls, a testimony to your goodness, that must be expressed.

Pastor: If only the lost and lonely and discouraged could know the depths of your love and your eternal concern for those who will follow you.

People: You have made everything beautiful in its time, O Lord, and placed eternity in our hearts. Yet, how shall we grasp its meaning and understand its importance?

Pastor: My songs are so often off-key.

People: Our speech is so inadequate to express how we feel.

Pastor: But the heavens declare the glory of God, and the earth beneath proclaims his wonderful works in the midst of men and women in every generation.

People: Even the songs of the birds give honor to your name, O Lord, and the trees stretch their branches toward your heavenly home.

Pastor: See God in the flowers that glow in their beauty, and in the changing colors of the seasons. Find him in the mountains and declare him in the valleys. Discern his vitality in the rapids and discover his majesty in the pounding surf that scours the ocean shore.

People: How glorious it is to be alive, O Lord, and to hear your praises sung throughout your creation. May every breath we draw be dedicated to the honor of your name.

Hymn: "Joyful, Joyful, We Adore Thee" Hymn To Joy

Alternate Hymn: "For The Beauty Of The Earth" Dix

Number 6

Praise Hymn: "This Is The Day" Les Garrett

Call To Worship

Pastor: "And God said, 'Let there be light,' and there was light. And God saw that the light was good; and God called the light day, and darkness he called night. And there was evening and there was morning, one day." *(Genesis 1:4ff RSV)*

People: "The heavens are telling the glory of God; and the firmament proclaims his handiwork. Day to day pours forth speech and night to night declares knowledge." *(Psalm 19:1ff RSV)*

Pastor: "Yours is the day, yours also the night; you established the luminaries and the sun." *(Psalm 74:16 NRSV)*

People: "By day the Lord commands his steadfast love, and at night his song is with me, a prayer to the God of my life." *(Psalm 42:8 RSV)*

Pastor: "This is the day which the Lord has made; let us rejoice and be glad in it." *(Psalm 118:24 RSV)*

People: "Every day I will bless you, and praise your name forever and ever. Great is the Lord; and greatly to be praised; his greatness is unsearchable." *(Psalm 145:2-3)*

Unison: "So teach us to number our days that we may gain a heart of wisdom." *(Psalm 90:12 RSV)*

Hymn: "O Day Of Rest And Gladness" Mendebras

Invocation and Lord's Prayer

Pastor: "He is the image of the invisible God, the firstborn over all creation."

People: We come to worship with a sense of awe.

Pastor: "For by him all things were created; things in heaven and on earth, visible and invisible, whether thrones or powers or rulers or authorities."

People: As we gather for worship, we must marvel at his majesty.

Pastor: "And he is the head of the body, the church. For God was pleased to have all his fullness dwell in him, and through him to reconcile to himself all things, whether things on earth or things in heaven, by making peace through his blood, shed on the cross."

People: We enter the sanctuary with a profound sense of humility.

Pastor: "Once you were alienated from God and were enemies in your minds because of your evil behavior. But now, he has reconciled you by Christ's physical body through death to present you holy in his sight, without blemish and free from accusation." *(Colossians 1:15ff)*

People: We come before our God with a sense of gratefulness in our hearts, and with praise on our lips.

Hymn: "Praise To The Lord, Almighty" Lebe Den Herren

Invocation and Lord's Prayer

Number 8

Pastor: "In the beginning ..."

People: "In the beginning was the Word"

Pastor: "In the beginning was the Word, and the Word was with God"

People: "In the beginning was the Word, and the Word was with God, and the Word was God."

Pastor: "The Word ..."

People: "The Word became flesh ..."

Pastor: "The Word became flesh and made his dwelling among us."

People: "We have seen his glory, the glory of the One and Only Begotten, who came from the Father, full of grace and truth."

Pastor: Praise God!

People: Praise God in the heavens and proclaim his glories to the ends of the earth! *(Taken from John 1:1ff, 1:14ff RSV)*

Hymn: "Crown Him With Many Crowns" Diademata

Alternate Hymn: "Join All The Glorious Names" Darwall's 148th

Invocation and Lord's Prayer

Number 9

Pastors: Teacher, instruct those who claim your name to keep silent.

People: To contain our speech is impossible, to withhold our praise is untenable.

Pastor: Rabbi, teach your followers proper decorum.

People: We must cry out, "Blessed is the Savior, who comes in the name of our God!" We must proclaim, "Peace in heaven and glory in the highest!"

Pastor: Teacher, rebuke your disciples!

People: Were we to keep silent, the very stones would cry out!

Hymn: "All Creatures Of Our God And King" Lasst Uns Erfreuen

Alternate Praise Hymn: "How Majestic Is Your Name" Michael W. Smith

Invocation and Lord's Prayer

2 — Calls To Worship With Praise And Celebration

Using Traditional Hymns And Praise Hymns

Number 10

Pastor: "In the beginning was the Word, and the Word was with God, and the Word was God."

People: *(To be sung)* **"Christ we do all adore thee, and we do praise thee forever."**

Pastor: "He was with God in the beginning. Through him all things were made; without him nothing was made that has been made."

People: *(To be sung)* **"Christ we do all adore thee, and we do praise thee forever. Christ we do all adore thee, and we do praise thee forever."**

Pastor: In him was life, and that life was the light of all peoples. The light shines in the darkness; but the darkness cannot overcome it." *(paraphrase of John 1:1-5 RSV)*

People: *(To be Sung)* **"Christ we do all adore thee, and we do praise thee forever. Christ we do all adore thee, and we do praise thee forever. For on the cross hast thou the world from sin redeemed. Christ, we do all adore thee, and we do praise thee forever."*****

Pastor: "In these last days God has spoken to us by his Son, whom he appointed heir of all things, and through whom he made the universe. The Son is the radiance of God's glory and the exact representation of his being, sustaining all things by his powerful word." *(Hebrews 1:2-3 RSV)*

People: Praise to God almighty, and to his Son and our Savior, Jesus Christ, in whom the fullness of God's revelation dwells. We have come to worship the God of glory, and to proclaim our salvation through our Lord Jesus Christ.

Hymn: "Praise The Lord, His Glories Show" Llanfair

Alternate Praise Hymn: "Sing Hallelujah" Linda Stassen

Invocation and Lord's Prayer

*"**Christ We Do All Adore Thee**" Adore Thee

Number 11

Pastor: Come all you who love the Lord, come into the sanctuary to worship our God. Come join your voices to declare the wondrous love which our Creator has shown to his children through all generations!

People: *(To be sung)* **"All glory, laud, and honor to thee, Redeemer, King, to whom the lips of children made sweet hosannas ring: Thou art the King of Israel, thou art David's royal Son, who in the Lord's name comest, the King and blessed One!"**

Pastor: All of creation joins together to declare the glory of the Lord. The trees of the forests adorn themselves in green and golden brown; the stars in the sky shine forth in their brightness; the attendants of heaven array themselves before the throne of God to proclaim his goodness!

People: *(To be sung)* **"The company of angels are praising thee on high, and mortal men and all things created made reply: The people of the Hebrews with palms before thee went; our praise and prayer and anthems before thee we present."**

Pastor: The gifts of God to his creation are many: the snow in the mountains to water the earth; new generations of every species to replenish the planet and bring renewal of life; and especially, the gift of many melodies to sing our praises and describe the joy of our hearts, for knowing something of the majesty of God.

People: *(To be sung)* **"To thee, before thy passion, they sang their hymns of praise; to thee, now high exalted, our melody we raise: thou didst accept their praises — accept the praise we bring, who in all good delightest, thou good and gracious King!"***

Pastor: With thanksgiving in our hearts, we stand in the holy courts of the Divine Ruler of the universe, and dare to open our mouths in praise of the Redeemer of all humankind. By

23

invitation of the Savior, we stand in the presence of the Author of Life, the Fount of All Knowledge, the Source of Love. We join in the everlasting song that proclaims the glory of the One who is crowned, Lord of all.

Hymn: "All Hail The Power Of Jesus' Name" Coronation

Invocation and Lord's Prayer

*"**All Glory, Laud, And Honor**" St. Theodulph

People: *(To be sung)* **"This is my Father's world, and to my listening ears, all nature sings, and 'round me rings the music of the spheres. This is my Father's world, I rest me in the thought of rocks and trees, of skies and seas — his hand the wonders wrought."**

Pastor: In the beginning, God had a plan for this world. He saw the glorious picture of all things beautiful and in their place. Moonbeams and puppy dogs, daffodils and people, everything was part of that extraordinary mosaic.

People: But the world did not remain together. We ripped ourselves apart. Adam and Eve tore themselves apart like a puzzle. Today, nations are tearing themselves apart.

West Side: Family and friends tear themselves apart.

East Side: Races and cultures tear away from each other into little pieces.

People: Some days, inside ourselves, we feel like a 500-piece puzzle, with no tabs and slots connected; and we need help.

Pastor: Jesus Christ came into our world to reassemble our puzzle pieces. Out of the pieces he shall create peace. Out of the brokenness he shall create wholeness. Out of the estrangement he shall fashion sisters and brothers in the Lord. Each of us is a puzzle piece that fits together with other pieces. As we connect in Jesus Christ, a beautiful picture of holy love is revealed, and all the earth shall celebrate.

People: *(To be sung)* **"This is my Father's world, the birds their carols raise, the morning light, the lily white, declare their Maker's praise. This is my Father's world: he shines in all that's fair; in the rustling grass I hear him pass, he speaks to me everywhere. This is my Father's world, O let me ne'er forget, that though the wrong seems oft so strong, God is the ruler yet. This is my Father's world: the battle is not done; Jesus who died shall be satisfied, and earth and heaven be one."***

25

Pastor: As we come together in worship, we come seeking union in the Spirit, that we may be united in our hearts and in our purpose to serve our God.

People: As you are the one God and Father of us all, make us one in you, that we may lift up our voices as one in prayer and praise of your goodness to us.

Invocation and Lord's Prayer

Hymn of Celebration: "We Are One In The Spirit" St. Brendan's

*"This Is My Father's World" Terra Beata

Number 13

Pastor: "How lovely is your dwelling place, O Lord of hosts! My soul longs, indeed it faints for the courts of the Lord; my heart and my flesh sing for joy to the living God." *(Psalm 84:1ff NRSV)*

People: *(To be sung)* *("majesty"* ~~copy in "We Have Come Into His~~ House"* verse 1 Bruce Ballinger)

Pastor: "Even the sparrow finds a home, and the swallow a nest for herself, where she may lay her young at your altars, O Lord of hosts, my King and my God. Happy are those who live in your house, ever singing your praise."

People: *(To be sung)* *(copy in "Majesty"* ~~"We Have Come Into His House" verse 2)~~

Pastor: "For a day in your courts is better than a thousand elsewhere. I would rather be a doorkeeper in the house of my God than dwell in the tents of wickedness. For the Lord God is a sun and shield; he bestows favor and honor. No good thing does the Lord withhold from those who walk uprightly."

People: *(To be sung)* *(copy in "Majesty"* ~~"We Have Come Into His House" verse 3)~~

Pastor: "Make a joyful noise to the Lord all the earth. Worship the Lord with gladness; come into his presence with singing! Enter his gates with thanksgiving, and his courts with praise. For the Lord is good; his steadfast love endures forever, and his faithfulness to all generations." *(Psalm 100 NRSV)*

People: *(To be sung)* *(copy in "Majesty"* ~~Jack Hayford)~~

Invocation and Lord's Prayer

Hymn of Celebration: "The Family Of God" *(Refrain only) (Family of God)*

*Include CCLI Number

Number 14

Pastor: "Have you not known? Have you not heard? Has it not been told to you from the beginning? Have you not understood from the foundations of the earth? It is he who sits above the circle of the earth, and its inhabitants are like grasshoppers; who stretches out in the heavens like a curtain, and spreads them like a tent to dwell in; who brings princes to nought, and makes the rulers of the earth as nothing." *(Isaiah 40:21ff RSV)*

People: *(To be sung)* **"Sing praise to God who reigns above, the God of all creation, the God of power, the God of love, the God of our salvation; with healing balm my soul he fills, and every faithless murmur skills: To God all praise and glory."**

Pastor: "To whom then will you compare me, that I should be like him? says the Holy One. Lift up your eyes on high and see: who created these? He who brings out their host by number, calling them all by name; by the greatness of his might, and because he is strong in power, not one is missing."

People: *(To be sung)* **"What God's almighty power hath made his gracious mercy keepeth; by morning glow or evening shade his watchful eye ne'er sleepeth; within the kingdom of his might, Lo! all is just and all is right: to God all praise and glory."**

Pastor: "The Lord is the everlasting God, the Creator of the ends of the earth. He does not faint or grow weary, his understanding is unsearchable. As we wait upon the Lord, he shall renew our strength, we shall mount up with wings and soar like the eagles, we shall run and not be weary, we shall walk and not faint."

People: *(To be sung)* **"The Lord is never far away, but, through all grief distressing, an ever present help and stay, our peace, and joy, and blessing; as with a mother's tender hand, he leads his own, his chosen band: to God all praise and glory.**

"Thus, all my gladsome way along, I sing aloud his praises, that men may hear the grateful song my voice unwearied raises, be joyful in the Lord, my heart, both soul and body bear your part: to God all praise and glory."*

Invocation and Lord's Prayer

*"**Sing Praise To God Who Reigns Above**" Mit Freuden Zart

Number 15

Pastor: "The heavens declare the glory of God; the skies proclaim the work of his hands.

People: "Day after day they pour forth speech; night after night they display knowledge."

Hymn: *(copy in v. 1, "We Sing The Greatness Of Our God"*, Lobe Den Herren)*

Pastor: "In the heavens he has pitched a tent for the sun,

People: "Which is like a bridegroom coming forth from his pavilion, like a champion rejoicing to run his course.

Pastor: "It rises at one end of the heavens and makes its circuit to the other;

People: "Nothing is hidden from its light."

Hymn: *(copy in v. 2, "We Sing The Greatness Of Our God")*

Pastor: "The law of the Lord is perfect, reviving the soul.

People: "The statutes of the Lord are trustworthy, making wise the simple.

Pastor: "The precepts of the Lord are right, giving joy to the heart.

People: "The commands of the Lord are radiant, giving light to the eyes.

Pastor: "The fear of the Lord is pure, enduring forever.

People: "The ordinances of the Lord are sure and altogether righteous.

Pastor: "By them is your servant warned;

People: "In keeping them there is great reward.

Unison: "May the words of our mouths and the meditations of our hearts be pleasing in your sight, O Lord, our rock and our redeemer." *(Psalm 19 RSV)*

Hymn: *(copy in v. 3, "We Sing The Greatness Of Our God")*

Pastor: We have come to worship today to be reminded of the holy law which is written on our hearts.

People: We have come together in worship to sing our praises to the God whose goodness pours out upon those who proclaim his name.

Invocation and Lord's Prayer

*Include CCLI Number

Number 16

Praise: *(To be sung) (copy in "We Will Glorify"* Twila Paris)*

Pastor: "O Lord, our Lord, how glorious is your name throughout the earth! Your splendor surpasses the heavens. From the lips of children and infants you have ordained praise that silences the enemy and gives rout to the avenger."

People: *(To be sung)* "O Worship The King" (v. 1 Lyons)
"O worship the King all glorious above, and gratefully sing his wonderful love; our shield and defender, the ancient of days, pavilioned in splendor and girded with praise."

Pastor: When I consider the magnificence of your heavens, and the work of your hands, the moon and the stars which you have set into place, what is a man that you are mindful of him? What is a woman that you care for her? And yet, you have made them in your image, and you have crowned them with glory and honor.

People: *(To be sung)* "O Worship The King" (v. 2)
"Frail children of dust, and feeble as frail, in thee do we trust, nor find thee to fail; thy mercies how tender, how firm to the end, our maker, defender, redeemer and friend."

Pastor: You have given them dominion over all the earth; you have put everything under their feet: all the flocks and herds and beasts of the field; all the birds that fill the air, and fish teeming in the sea. O Lord, our Lord, how majestic is your name throughout all the earth. *(paraphrase of Psalm 8)*

People: *(To be sung)* "O Worship The King" (vv. 3, 4)
"O tell of his might and sing of his grace, whose robe is the light, whose canopy space; his chariots of wrath the deep thunder clouds form, and dark is his path on the wings of the storm.

"Thy bountiful care what tongue can recite? It breathes in the air, it shines in the light, it streams from the hills, it descends to the plain, and sweetly distills in the dew and the rain."

Invocation and Lord's Prayer

Hymn of Celebration: "Great Is The Lord" Michael W. Smith, Deborah D. Smith

***Include CCLI Number**

Number 17

Pastors: "Make a joyful noise to the Lord, all the lands! Serve the Lord with gladness! Come into his presence with singing!"

People: *(To be sung)* "Praise to the Lord, the almighty, the King of creation!"

Pastor: "Know that the Lord is God! It is he who has made us, and we are his; we are his people, and the sheep of his pasture."

People: *(To be sung)* "O my soul, praise him, for he is thy health and salvation."

Pastor: "Enter his gates with thanksgiving, and his courts with praise! Give thanks to him and bless his name!"

People: *(To be sung)* "All ye who hear, now to his temple draw near;"

Pastor: "For the Lord is good; his steadfast love endures forever, and his faithfulness to all generations." *(Psalm 100 RSV)*

People: *(To be sung)* "Join me in glad adoration." *(Continue to sing final three verses below.)* "Praise to the Lord, who o'er all things so wondrously reigneth, shelters thee under thy wings, yes, so gently sustaineth! Hast thou not seen how all thy longings have been, granted in what he ordaineth?

"Praise to the Lord, who doth prosper thy work and defend thee; surely his goodness and mercy here daily attend thee. Ponder anew what the Almighty can do, if with his love he befriend thee.

"Praise to the Lord! O let all that is in me adore him! All that hath life and breath, come now with praises before him. Let the amen, sound from his people again: gladly for aye we adore him."*

Invocation and Lord's Prayer

*"Praise To The Lord, The Almighty" Lobe Den Herren

34

Number 18

Pastor: We praise you, O Lord. From everlasting to everlasting, yours is the greatness and the power and the glory and the majesty and the splendor; for all that is and ever has been, is yours. You, O Lord, are the exalted head over all; and we praise your most holy name.

People: *(To be sung) (copy in "Glorify Thy Name"* Donna Adkins)*

Pastor: "Let the same mind be in you that was in Christ Jesus, who, though he was in the form of God, did not regard equality with God as something to be exploited, but emptied himself, taking the form of a servant. And being found in human form, he humbled himself and became obedient to the point of death — even death on a cross. Therefore, God also highly exalted him and gave him the name that is above every name, so that at the name of Jesus every knee should bend, and every tongue confess that Jesus Christ is Lord, to the glory of God the Father." *(Philippians 2:5-11 NRSV)*

People: *(To be sung) (copy in "Glorify Thy Name," substituting "Jesus" for "Father")*

Pastor: Therefore, brothers and sisters, in Christ you and I are set free to live lives that please our Lord. For as we are led by the Spirit of God, we are known as children of God. And when we cry out "Abba! Father!" it is the Holy Spirit bearing witness with our spirits that we are children of God — heirs of God, and heirs of Christ, as we are bound together in the Holy Spirit. *(paraphrase of Romans 8:12ff)*

People: *(To be sung) (copy in "Glorify Thy Name," substituting "Spirit" for "Father")*

Pastor: Jesus Christ is the foundation stone which was earlier rejected, but is that stone upon which we must build our lives. There is salvation in no one else; for there is no other name under heaven given in all humanity, whereby men and women might be saved. *(paraphrase Acts 4:11, 12)*

35

People: *(To be sung) (copy in "His Name Is Wonderful"* Audrey Meier)*

Invocation and Lord's Prayer

Hymn of Celebration: "Join All The Glorious Names" Darwall's 148th

Alternate Praise Hymn: "Emmanuel" Bob McGee

*Include CCLI Number

Number 19

Pastor: "Who shall ascend the hill of the Lord? And who shall stand in his holy place?"

People: "Have mercy on me, O God, according to thy steadfast love; according to thy abundant mercy blot out my transgressions."

Pastor: "He who has clean hands and a pure heart, who does not lift up his soul to what is false, and does not swear deceitfully."

People: "Wash me thoroughly from my iniquity, and cleanse me from my sin!"

Pastor: "He will receive blessing from the Lord, and vindication from the God of his salvation."

People: "Create in me a clean heart, O God, and put a new and right spirit within me."

Pastor: "Lift up your heads, O Gates"

People: "And be lifted up, O ancient doors! that the King of glory may come in.

Pastor: "Who is the King of glory?

People: "The strong and mighty, the Lord of hosts, he is the King of glory!" *(Psalms 24 and 51 RSV)*

Hymn: "Lift Up Your Heads, Ye Mighty Gates" Truro

Invocation and Lord's Prayer

Number 20

Pastor: Let us come together in worship and open our hearts to the good news: "Jesus Christ is the image of the invisible God, the first-born of all creation; for in him all things were created in heaven and on earth, visible and invisible, whether thrones or dominions or principalities or authorities .... For in Jesus Christ all the fullness of God was pleased to dwell, and through him to reconcile to himself all things, whether on earth or in heaven, making peace by the blood of his cross." *(Colossians 1:15ff RSV)*

People: (To be sung) "Jesus Saves" (William Kirkpatrick) **"We have heard the joyful sound: Jesus saves! Jesus saves! Spread the tidings all around: Jesus saves! Jesus saves! Bear the news to every land, climb the steeps and cross the waves; Onward! 'tis the Lord's command; Jesus saves! Jesus saves!"**

Pastor: "In this the love of God was made manifest among us, that God sent his Son into the world, so that we might live through him. In this is love, not that we loved God, but that he loved us and sent his Son to be the expiation for our sins." *(1 John 4:9ff)*

People: *(To be sung)* **"Waft it on the rolling tide: Jesus saves! Jesus saves! Tell to sinners far and wide: Jesus saves! Jesus saves! Sing, ye islands of the sea; Echo back, ye ocean caves; Earth shall keep her jubilee: Jesus saves! Jesus saves!"**

Pastor: "Those who believe in the Son of God have the testimony in their hearts ... And this is the testimony: God gave us eternal life, and this life is in his Son. Whoever has the Son has life; whoever does not have the Son of God does not have life." *(1 John 5:10ff NRSV)*

People: *(To be sung)* **"Sing above the battle strife: Jesus saves! Jesus saves! By his death and endless life: Jesus saves! Jesus saves! Sing it softly through the gloom, when the heart for mercy craves; sing in triumph o'er the tomb: Jesus saves! Jesus saves!"**

Pastor: Therefore, we come together in this hour, to claim our salvation in the Lord, to reaffirm the gift of life granted to us through Jesus Christ our Lord, and to open our hearts further to the saving knowledge of the One who calls us to live daily, under the empowerment of the Holy Spirit.

People: *(To be sung)* **"Give the winds a mighty voice: Jesus saves! Jesus saves! Let the nations now rejoice: Jesus saves! Jesus saves! Shout salvation full and free, highest hills and deepest caves; this our song of victory: Jesus saves! Jesus saves!"***

Invocation and Lord's Prayer

Hymn of Celebration: "Victory In Jesus" Hartford

*"Jesus Saves" William Kirkpatrick

Number 21

Pastor: We have gathered in the sanctuary of the Most High to worship him and to praise his holy name.

People: We have come together to adore the Lord our God, to pray that we may receive a word from his Living Word.

Pastor: But we cannot worship on our own. For unless he aids us in our adoration, we will not be able to wholly reach out to him.

People: *(To be sung) (copy in "Brethren We Have Met To Worship"* Holy Manna)*

Pastor: Worship is not entertainment. Worship is involvement. Worship is participating with God in his many acts of salvation; it is equipping ourselves for working in the kingdom on earth; it is bearing witness to the mighty acts of God in the human community; it is standing in awe of judgments, mercy, and redemptive love.

People: *(To be sung) (copy in "Bless His Holy Name"* Andrae Crouch)*

Invocation and Lord's Prayer

*Include CCLI Number

3 — Calls To Worship
Relating A Story

Number 22

Leader: "But joy comes with the morning!"

People: What does that mean, "But joy comes with the morning?"

Leader: The psalmist has spoken of stress and enemies, of pain and the threats of hell itself. He tells of the anguish of the soul, and the demands of a God who loves him, but demands accountability of him. He says, "Weeping may tarry for the night, but joy comes with the morning." *(Psalm 30:5 RSV)*

People: We know what that psalmist was speaking about; we've walked his road with him. His stress and temptations have been ours; and his confrontations with the evil one are similar to those that have plagued us. We too have experienced tears in the night.

Leader: But don't stop there. The world puts a period after the weeping in the night. The psalmist knew a great truth; he used a comma and continued: "but joy comes with the morning!"

Hymn: "When Morning Gilds The Skies" Laudes Domini

Invocation and Lord's Prayer

Number 23

Pastor: In the year King Uzziah died, the Lord was sitting upon a throne, high and lifted up; and his train filled the temple.

People: An awesome sight! A wondrous sight! A fearful sight!

Pastor: Above him stood the seraphim; each had six wings: with two he covered his face, with two he covered his feet, and with two he flew.

People: Woe is me! I am lost! My lips are unclean. By your holy presence, I stand convicted of my sins.

Pastor: And one seraphim called to another and said, "Holy, holy, holy is the Lord of hosts; the whole earth is full of his glory!" *(based on Isaiah 6:1ff)*

People: With contrite hearts, O God, we ask to be cleansed of unrighteousness. Through your mercy we receive your steadfast love.

Pastor: As we come to worship, God redeems us and calls us to do his will. The foundation of the altar shook as that heavenly voice called out: "Whom shall I send, and who will go for us?"

People: Paul answered the call, and Esther; Abraham embraced the command, and Mary humbled herself.

Pastor: And what of this generation? Are you willing to be obedient?

People: We enter into the Lord's courts with praise; and we ask for the courage, when the call comes, to say, "Here am I! Send me."

Number 24

(In conjunction with celebration of the Lord's Supper)

Pastor: We gather today, as the disciples gathered, and will soon join them around the table of our Lord. Each came with his own agenda in mind; each was preoccupied with his own fears and concerns and goals.

People: Sometimes we come to worship out of the fashion of it, sometimes for fellowship, sometimes to receive spiritual nourishment. We too have our own agendas; we are concerned about our needs and our dreams.

Pastor: In the midst of the proceedings, Jesus disrupted a very nice religious dinner by getting up, taking off his outer robe, kneeling down, and commencing to wash the disciples' feet.

People: A most disconcerting deed!

Pastor: A most perplexing action on the part of the honored host!

People: What were they to make of this effrontery to their pride?

Pastor: Then Jesus took his place at the table and asked his stunned friends, "Do you understand what I have done?"

People: Obviously they did not understand.

Pastor: And do you understand? In the midst of stress and violence and power games of every kind, do you understand the meaning of Jesus, whom we call Lord, washing feet?

People: It doesn't fit the standards of this world. But we have come to worship today with the prayer that our Lord will help us to understand his humility, his love, and his victory over the world, that we too might be victorious in the living of our days.

Hymn: "My Tribute" Andrae Crouch

Invocation and Lord's Prayer

Number 25

Pastor: Jesus went to Simon's house for dinner.

People: Simon must have felt honored to host such a popular guest.

Pastor: Yes. But his party was disrupted by a disheveled woman who had no regard for common rules of propriety. Simon was both indignant and embarrassed.

People: We too are embarrassed by people who come to our parties and don't play by the rules.

Pastor: There's more to it than that. Jesus honored her more than he honored Simon, his host. She had gained spiritual insights that the most religious people present had missed.

Are you here today as Simon, or as the disheveled woman? As the one who is self-assured and doesn't need anything from the Lord? Or, as the one who is totally broken in spirit and utterly dependent upon God's grace? *(story found in Luke 7:36ff)*

People: We should be here as the woman came. More often, we're here as Simon. Lord, teach us about humility and the wonder of your grace. Amen.

Hymn: "Wonderful Grace Of Jesus" Wonderful Grace

Invocation and Lord's Prayer

Number 26

Pastor: Water!

People: Water?

Pastor: Water! Come to the water, all of you who thirst. "With joy, you will draw water from the wells of salvation."

People: We come as the Samaritan woman came to the well, petitioning Jesus: "Sir, give us this water, that we may not thirst again."

Pastor: Jesus pointed out to the woman that she did not fully understand his offer.

People: And we also are sometimes bewildered by his teachings and confused by his call upon our lives. But we are here to receive that living refreshment for our souls that only the Lord, "the fountain of living water" can provide.

Pastor: The Spirit and the Bride say, "Come." Let him who is thirsty come; let her who desires, take the water of life without price. Then shall it come to pass, as Jesus proclaimed: "He who believes in me, as scripture has said, 'Out of his heart shall flow rivers of living water.' "

People: And we shall be like that tree planted by the water, that sends out its roots by the stream, and does not fear when the heat comes, for even in drought, it shall not cease to bear fruit. *(Excerpts from Isaiah 12:3; Jeremiah 17:8, 13; John 3:5, 4:13, 7:37; Revelation 22:17)*

Hymn: "Come To The Water" Children of the Day

Alternate Hymn: "Rejoice, Ye Pure In Heart" Marion

Invocation and Lord's Prayer

Number 27

Pastor: The flinty rock is unforgiving, the scrub brush is sparse, and the shepherd and his sheep must travel far and wide for forage. It's lonely and isolating work. Finding water, protecting one's self from the heat, keeping a watchful eye for predators. It's all in a day's work. And then ... a bush, a bush engulfed by fire but is not consumed!

People: What is this wonder that catches the eye? In the midst of the wilderness, in the middle of a work-a-day world, his life is invaded!

Pastor: Moses turns aside to examine a bush that will not disintegrate in the flames, and discovers God. And that which was common sand and desert scrub, has suddenly become a sanctuary, the dwelling place of God.

People: "Moses. Do not come any closer!" God said. "Take off your sandals, for the place where you are standing is holy ground!"

Solo or Duet: "Holy Ground" (v. 1) by Christopher Beatty

Pastor: "I have seen the suffering of my people. I am sending you to Pharaoh to bring my people, the Israelites, out of Egypt."

Men: Moses wasn't seeking God. God was seeking him.

Women: He was given a commission he didn't want.

People: But when he opened his life to the will and calling of God, he became an instrument of holy power that shook the world, reshaped history, and saved the people of God.

Solo or Duet: "Holy Ground" (v. 2) by Christopher Beatty

People: As Moses came before the burning bush and found himself in the temple of your presence, so do we come this morning into your presence, O God, praising you and offering ourselves to your leading, that the cries of the hungry

may not go unheeded, the anguish of the captives may be addressed, and the message of salvation may be proclaimed through our faithfulness today. Amen.

Solo or Duet: "Holy Ground" by Geron Davis

Invocation and Lord's Prayer

Number 28

Pastor: You've met Martha before: the consummate organizer, the immaculate housekeeper, the perpetual motion machine who must always keep her hands busy; the personnel director who has jobs, without end, for everyone in the vicinity.

People: We know her. Some of us bear her name; some of us are driven to the edge by her insistent demands upon us, who are less task oriented.

Pastor: Much is accomplished by the Marthas of the world.

People: True. But maybe, what she is accomplishing would be more meaningful if she took time out for some reflection, occasionally.

Pastor: Now you're onto something important. Martha was busy with many things, and upset that others were not equally in turmoil. "Martha, Martha," said Jesus, "you are anxious and troubled about many things. One thing is needful." Her sister Mary had chosen the better portion: to sit quietly at the feet of Jesus, enjoy his fellowship, learn his ways, respond to his teachings, and receive his peace.

People: Lord, as we come before you in worship this morning, help us to put away our busyness and those things which distract, that we may draw close to you and enjoy your fellowship, learn your ways, respond to your teachings, and receive your peace. Amen.

Hymn: "Near To The Heart Of God" McAfee

Invocation and Lord's Prayer

Number 29

Pastor: The ground was dry and the sky was blue, only the barest breeze rustled the grasses, as the axe was applied to the tree.

People: It was a day like any other: babies cried, mothers sighed, children fussed at their chores.

Pastor: The sheep grazed nearby that day as they had done the day before. But on that day, they nibbled to the rhythm of the saw that fashioned the planks.

People: The men engaged in business and dreamed of victory over their foes; it was a season like any season — unremarkable to the casual observer.

Pastor: Night followed day and day followed night, as the lonely hammer drove the pegs home.

People: For sin stalked the land and infected the hearts of women and men, as a dark spirit clouded the souls of the people of earth.

Pastor: The clouds dotted the horizon and drifted eastward, as the smell of hot pitch filled the air.

People: Who would be found faithful in the land, and who would seek the Light Of Life in the midst of the darkness? None but one man and woman and their offspring, standing in faith, working in obedience when the eye could find no proof to vindicate such apparent foolishness.

Pastor: They looked to Jehovah and were faithful to their charge. And in that barren land, found salvation on the day that the rains came down.

People: On this day of worship, in a land that is yet dark with sin, guide us, O Great Jehovah, to the Light Of Life, that we may be saved from the flood, that we may know salvation, and that we may be a witness for your redeeming love, even when the eye can find no proof to vindicate such faith.

Hymn: "My Shepherd Will Supply My Need" Resignation

Alternate Hymn: "My Faith Has Found A Resting Place" No Other Plea

Invocation and Lord's Prayer

Number 30

Pastor: As we come before the Lord this morning, let us come as Hannah came. Her heart was heavy, her life had become an unbearable burden. That for which she yearned more than for life itself, seemed to be withheld from her by God. She was bewildered, hurt, perplexed, yet hopeful, as she entered the house of the Lord.

People: We too have felt the pain and carried the burden. We also have yearned to know the will of God and receive the gift for which we have earnestly prayed.

Pastor: Hannah was ridiculed by her neighbors, and scorned by her friends. The arrows of mockery found their way to her heart, and the agony of her soul poured out at the altar of the Lord.

People: And we have come to the house of the Lord, as well. As we search our souls, we remember our own yearnings and pains, our petitions and dreams. We too can number the things that God has granted us, and the things which he has withheld.

Pastor: Then came Hannah to the altar, and there she opened her life to God, where he might see the secrets of her heart, and respond to the deepest needs of her being.

People: *(To be sung)* **"Search me, O God, and know my heart today; try me, O Savior, know my thoughts, I Pray. See if there be some wicked way in me; cleanse me from every sin, and set me free.**

"I praise thee, Lord, for cleansing me from sin; fulfill thy Word and make me pure within. Fill me with fire, where once I burned with shame; grant my desire to magnify thy name."*

Pastor: Here was the secret to Hannah's spiritual success. The life she sought from God, the gift for which she yearned with all her heart, she dedicated back to God before she received it. She would ask for no gift from God that she would not offer back to him for use in his service. Here is a model

51

for us, as we come to worship God and set before him our petitions. How far are we willing to go to dedicate back to him those things which we seek from him?

People: *(To be sung)* **"Lord take my life, and make it wholly thine; fill my poor heart with thy great love divine. Take all my will, my passion, self and pride; I now surrender, Lord — in me abide."**

Pastor: And a son was granted to Hannah. His name was Samuel. And this joy-filled mother brought her babe to the temple to dedicate him and give thanks: "My heart delights in the Lord; my strength is exalted in my God. I rejoice in the salvation you have granted me! There is none holy like the Lord. There is no rock like our God!" *(1 Samuel 2:1-2 NIV)*

Hymn: "O Worship The King" Lyons

Invocation and Lord's Prayer

Hymn of Celebration: "Behold What Manner Of Love" Patricia Van Tine

*__"Cleanse Me"__ Maori

Number 31

Pastor: An angel of the Lord appeared to the shepherds and the glory of the Lord shone round about him. "Be not afraid!" cried the angel; "For I bring you good tidings of great joy! To you is born this day, in the city of David, A Savior, who is Christ the Lord!" *(Luke 2:9ff RSV)*

People: *(To be sung)* **"All hail the power of Jesus' name! Let angels prostrate fall; bring forth the royal diadem, and crown him Lord of all; bring forth the royal diadem, and crown him Lord of all!"**

Pastor: Jesus came from Galilee to the Jordan to be baptized by John. And when Jesus was baptized, behold, the heavens were opened and he saw the Spirit of God descending like a dove, and alighting on him; and lo, a voice from heaven said, "this is my Son, with whom I am well pleased!" *(Matthew 3:13ff RSV)*

People: *(To be sung)* **"Ye chosen seed of Israel's race, ye ransomed from the fall, hail him who saves you by his grace, and crown him Lord of all; hail him who saves you by his grace, and crown him Lord of all!"**

Pastor: Jesus took Peter, James, and John high up on the mountain. And he was transfigured before them, and his face shone like the sun, and his garments became white as light. And behold, there appeared to them Moses and Elijah, talking with him. And lo, a bright cloud overshadowed them, and a voice from the cloud said, "This is my beloved Son, with whom I am well pleased. Listen to him!" *(Matthew 17:1ff RSV)*

People: *(To be sung)* **"Let every kindred, every tribe, on this terrestrial ball, to him all majesty ascribe, and crown him Lord of all; to him all majesty ascribe, and crown him Lord of all!"**

Pastor: And Peter said: "For we made known to you the power and coming of our Lord Jesus Christ. We were eye witnesses

53

to his majesty. When he received honor and glory from God the Father, we heard the voice which was borne to him by the majestic glory, as we stood upon that mountain. You will do well to pay attention to this as to a lamp shining in a dark place, until the day dawns and the Morning Star rises in your hearts." *(2 Peter 1:16ff RSV)*

People: *(To be sung)* **"O that with yonder sacred throng we at his feet may fall! We'll join the everlasting song, and crown him Lord of all; we'll join the everlasting song, and crown him Lord of all!"***

Invocation and Lord's Prayer

Hymn of Celebration: "Crown Him With Many Crowns" Diademata

***"All Hail The Power Of Jesus' Name"** Coronation

4 — Calls To Worship
With A Commitment Theme

Number 32

Pastor: Choose ye!

People: Choose ye this day!

Pastor: Choose ye this day whom you shall serve!

People: As for me and my house, we will serve the Lord God!

Unison: *(To be sung) (Insert words to "I Will Serve Thee" William J. Gaither)*

Pastor: When we come before the Lord, he will receive us in love; he offers to redeem us of our sins; and he šets before us a new opportunity, which we may choose, that will enrich our lives in the Spirit. "Enter his gates with thanksgiving and his courts with praise," that you may receive the blessings that God has for you today.

Unison: *(To be sung) (Insert words to "We Have Come Into His House" Bruce Ballinger)*

Invocation and Lord's Prayer

Hymn of Celebration: "Rejoice, The Lord Is King" Darwall's 148th

Number 33

Pastor: Jesus told the paralytic to rise, take up his bed, and walk. The angel told Philip to rise and go to the Gaza Road and witness to the Ethiopian. Jesus told Saul of Tarsus to rise and go into the city and prepare to be the world's greatest evangelist. The Lord told Peter to rise, and go as a missionary to the Gentiles.

Men: Rise up, O men of God! Have done with lesser things.

Women: Rise up, O women of God! To serve the King of kings.

Men: Rise up, O men of God! The church for you does wait.

Women: Rise up, O women of God! Rise up and make her great.

Men: Rise up, O men of God! Tread where his feet have trod.

Unison: As brothers and sisters of the Son, rise up, O men and women of God!

Hymn: "We Are God's People" Symphony

Alternate Hymn: "Renew Thy Church, Her Ministries Restore" All Is Well

Invocation and Lord's Prayer

*Words adapted from "Rise Up, O Men Of God" by William P. Merrill

Number 34

Hymn: *(copy in "My Father Watches Over Me"* v. 1, and refrain; C. H. Gabriel)*

Pastor: Whom do you trust?

People: That's a hard question to answer. We're told to trust our government, our teachers, our family members, our friends.

Pastor: But whom do you trust?

People: The Bible says, "Trust in the Lord with all thine heart; and lean not unto thine own understanding." *(Proverbs 3:5 KJV)*

Pastor: And yet the question remains: Whom do you trust?

People: The truth is, we trust very few people. Often, we don't really trust God to care or respond. And sometimes, we can barely trust ourselves.

Pastor: It's hard then, to follow the psalmist's challenge to "Commit your way to the Lord; trust in him, and he will act." *(Psalm 37:5)*

People: We should do it, we try. Occasionally we even succeed. But to trust openly, fully, completely — that takes more courage and faith than we possess on our own.

Pastor: Then as we gather for worship, we need to pray to receive the indwelling power of the Holy Spirit to give life to the words we sing: "I trust in God, I know he cares for me . . ."

Hymn: *(To be sung) (Copy in vv. 2, 3 and refrain of "My Father Watches Over Me")*

Invocation and Lord's Prayer

Hymn of Celebration: "Great Is Thy Faithfulness" Faithfulness

*Include CCLI Number

Number 35

Pastor: Hair!

People: Hair?

Pastor: Hair! Let's think about hair.

People: For some of us, there's not much to think about. For some of us, it's our crown. For most of us, it's something we fuss with a dozen times a day, and is the first thing which concerns us when we think about our appearance.

Pastor: Would you dry Jesus' feet with your hair — in public — in the presence of those people who already hold you in contempt — kneeling there with matted, muddied tresses, receiving the sneers of the guests?

People: We remember Mary doing that. She would have to be very focused to survive the humiliation.

Pastor: In fact, all who truly seek to honor the Lord, and worship him, must be very focused. Few people in the world will honor your devotion. Less will think highly of you for demonstrating a humble spirit.

People: Then our prayer must be that God will help us to focus on him this morning, as with humility, we come before the Lord in worship.

Unison: *(To be sung) (Copy in "Turn Your Eyes Upon Jesus"* Helen H. Lemmel — Refrain, vv. 1, 3, Refrain)*

Pastor: Light! Glory! Grace! Gifts of God beyond price! Come into his sanctuary to receive that which he has awaiting you in abundance. Sing praise to him, the God of our salvation!

Unison: *(To be sung)* "Sing Praise To God Who Reigns Above" Mit Freuden Zart

"Sing praise to God who reigns above, the God of all creation, the God of pow'r, the God of love, the God of our salvation; with healing balm my soul he fills, and every faithless murmur stills: To God all praise and glory.

"What God's almighty power hath made his gracious mercy keepeth; By morning glow or evening shade his watchful eye ne'er sleepeth; Within the kingdom of his might, lo! all is just and all is right: To God all praise and glory."

Invocation and Lord's Prayer

*Include CCLI Number

Number 36

Pastor: The kingdom of heaven is like a grain.

People: Like a pebble.

Pastor: Not that big.

People: Like a speck.

Pastor: That's more like it. The kingdom of heaven is like a mustard seed that is no bigger than a speck.

People: Like the tiniest dot of a seed that a farmer planted in his field.

Pastor: But there was life in that smallest of seeds.

People: And it grew, first as a sprout, then as a small plant, then as a great bush, where the birds of the air could roost.

Pastor: God is the farmer who has come today to plant seeds of faith and commitment, witness, and reconciliation. In services of worship, God is the sower of ideas and challenges that can grow us into beautiful lives of service which will provide refreshment and shelter for many.

People: As we come together for worship to pray and to sing praises, and to hear the Word of the Lord, we ask, O God, that you would prepare our souls for the planting, and lay within our hearts, seeds that will one day, bear much fruit. Amen.

Praise Hymn: copy in "Lord, Be Glorified"* Bob Kilpatrick

Pastor: Jesus tells us that the kingdom of heaven is in our midst. We are the Lord's fertile ground, the "demonstration plot" for the world, whereby he might show to an unbelieving generation how great is his redeeming love for those who call upon his holy name.

People: We come before you in praise and thanksgiving, and we open our lives to your Holy Spirit, that we may share with you in your redemptive work among the sons and daughters of humanity.

Invocation and Lord's Prayer

Hymn of Celebration: "In Moments Like These" David Graham

*Include CCLI Number

Number 37

Pastor: "Go ye."

People: "But how?"

Pastor: "Go ye into all the world and make disciples of all nations."

People: "But how are they to call on One in whom they have not believed?"

Pastor: "Baptize them in the name of the Father and of the Son and of the Holy Spirit."

People: "And how are they to believe in One whom they have never heard?"

Pastor: "Teaching them to observe all that I have commanded you."

People: "And how are they to hear without someone to proclaim him?"

Pastor: "And lo, I am with you always, to the close of the age." *(Matthew 28:18-20)*

People: "And how are they to proclaim him unless they are sent? As it is written, 'How beautiful are the feet of those who bring good news!' " *(Romans 10:14-15 NRSV)*

Hymn: "We've A Story To Tell To The Nations" Message

Pastor: When Isaiah entered the temple to worship God he was confronted.

People: He was confronted with his sin, as we are.

Pastor: And after his cleansing from sin, he was again confronted — confronted with a challenge to proclaim the Word of God to the nation, that all the people might be saved.

People: O God, we have come into the sanctuary today, risking confrontation with your holy will. Whether we are the ones

to be sent, or we are part of the support for those who are called, may we be found faithful, so that your word will indeed, go throughout the earth and bear much fruit for the kingdom.

Invocation and Lord's Prayer

Hymn of Consecration: "Renew Thy Church, Her Ministries Restore" All Is Well

Number 38

Pastor: "Come."

People: "Come unto me."

Pastor: "Come unto me, all who labor and are heavy laden, and I will give you rest."

People: *(To be sung) (copy in "Seek Ye First"* vv. 1 and 3, Karen Lafferty)*

Pastor: "Take my yoke upon you, and learn from me; for I am gentle and lowly in heart, and you will find rest for your souls. For my yoke is easy, and my burden is light." *(Matthew 11:29 RSV)*

People: *(To be sung) (copy in "Bind Us Together"* Bob Gilman)*

Invocation and Lord's Prayer

Hymn of Celebration: "We Are God's People" Symphony

*Include CCLI Number

Number 39

Pastor: In

People: In the beginning

Pastor: In the beginning God created

People: In the beginning was the Word

Pastor: In the beginning God created the heavens and the earth

People: In the beginning was the Word, and the Word was with God, and the Word was God.

Pastor: The earth was without form and void, and darkness was upon the face of the deep;

People: He was in the beginning with God; all things were made through him, and without him was not anything made that was made.

Pastor: And God said, "Let there be light!" And there was light.

People: The light shines in the darkness and the darkness has not overcome it.

Pastor: Who is the light?

People: Jesus said, "I am the Light of the World; he who follows me will not walk in darkness, but will have the light of life." *(John 8:12 RSV)*

Pastor: Then, as we come out of a world of sin and darkness, we gather to worship the Lord of light who has given substance and form to the universe and has established the light of life for our world, and the light of salvation for our souls. *(from Genesis 1:1ff and John 1:1ff RSV)*

Hymn: "We Sing The Greatness Of Our God" Ellacombe

Invocation and Lord's Prayer

Number 40

Pastor: Not only do I call you to worship this morning. More importantly, I call you to life eternal! Hear the promises from the Word of God. At the end of those days, the heavens will be shaken; and the signs of the Son of Man will appear in the sky, and all the tribes of earth shall mourn. We will see the Son of Man coming on the clouds of heaven with power and great glory! And he will send out his angels with a loud trumpet call, and they will gather his elect from the four winds! *(Matthew 24:30ff)*

People: *(To be sung) (copy in "Lo! He Comes With Clouds Descending"* vv. 1, 2 Regent Square)*

Pastor: "Lo! I tell you a mystery. We shall not all sleep, but we shall all be changed, in a moment in the twinkling of an eye, at the last trumpet." *(1 Corinthians 15:51)* For the Lord himself will descend from heaven with a cry, a command to the Archangel to sound the trumpet, so that we may be caught up together with the dead in Christ to meet our Lord in the air.

People: *(To be sung) (copy in "When We All Get To Heaven" refrain, v. 1, refrain Heaven)*

Pastor: "Then I saw a new heaven and a new earth; . . . And I saw the holy city, new Jerusalem, coming down out of heaven from God . . . and I heard a loud voice from the throne saying, "Behold, the dwelling of God is with those whom he loves. He will dwell with them and they shall be his people. God himself will wipe away every tear from their eyes, and death shall be no more. Neither will there be pain and remorse anymore. For all those things of old have passed away. All things have been made new." *(Revelation 21:1ff RSV)*

People: *(To be sung) (copy in "What A Day That Will Be"* What A Day)*

Pastor: In our celebration, there is also a warning. You must accept the gift of eternal life. For God shows his love for us in that while we were yet sinners, Christ died for us. Our justification comes through no works of our own, but through death and resurrection of Jesus Christ, whom we must claim as Lord. Perhaps that is your most important act of worship today.

People: *(To be sung) (copy in "For God So Loved The World"* Alfred B. Smith)*

Invocation and Lord's Prayer

*Include CCLI Number

5 — Calls To Worship Involving Personal Preparation

Number 41

This call to worship does not involve a litany. Rather, the pastor calls the congregation to a time of reflection upon what it costs them to worship. The following outline may be used or modified to suit individual purpose and style.

A. The cost of worship to David, who sinned against God by taking a census of the army
   1. A devastating plague descended upon the nation.
   2. David must be forgiven through a sacrifice he offers.
   3. He'll perform from the sacrifice on Araunah's threshing floor *(2 Samuel 24)*.
   4. Araunah offers to David, his yoke for the fire and his oxen for the sacrifice, at no cost to the king.
   5. David responds: "No, I insist on paying you for it. I will not sacrifice to the Lord my God, burnt offerings that cost me nothing."

B. The cost of worship to God, when we come before him
   1. He calls us to commitment.
   2. He must forgive us.
   3. He must exercise patience for our slow and indifferent hearts.
   4. His Son had to pay with his life for our salvation.

C. What does worship cost us today?
   1. Our time and money?
   2. Our freedom to enjoy our temptations?
   3. Our comfort, and maybe our spiritual innocence?

4. Our personal goals and value systems?
5. Society's affirmations and family support?

D. "I went to church one Sunday, and it cost me my life!"

Hymn: "Living For Jesus" Hendon

Alternate Hymn: " 'Are Ye Able?' Said The Master" Beacon Hill

Alternate Hymn: "Glorious Is Thy Name, Most Holy" Holy Manna

Prayer and Invocation

Number 42

This call to worship does not begin with a litany. Rather, the pastor calls the congregation to a time of personal reflection. The following outline may be used or modified to suit individual purpose and style. The congregation responds by singing one verse of "Cleanse Me," or another appropriate hymn, between each reflection.

Reflections Upon Worship
    A. How shall we come to worship today?
       1. What do we need to leave at the door, as we enter the sanctuary?
       2. Of what do we need to be forgiven?
       3. What parts of our lives need to be opened to God's healing light?

    B. Scripture: Matthew 5:21-24

Hymn: "Cleanse Me"* (v. 1 J. Edwin Orr)

Reflections Upon Worship
    A. It's not enough to create a vacuum, by ridding ourselves of the unholy features of our lives.
       1. We can empty our house of all our sins, we can wipe the slate clean.
       2. But an empty life, like an empty drawer, collects junk.

    B. Scripture: Luke 11:24-26

Hymn: "Cleanse Me" (v. 3)

Litany of Praise

Pastor: Cleansed of our sins, and surrendered to his will, we come before our God with praise on our lips.

People: We will boast in the Lord from the depths of our souls; let those who are hurting hear and rejoice. Together we will glorify the Lord, and exalt his name with one voice.

Pastor: As we seek the Lord he answers us, and he delivers us from all our fears.

People: As we look upon the God who saves us, our faces become radiant and they need never be covered with shame.

Pastor: The poor man called, and the Lord heard him; he saved him out of all his troubles.

People: The sinful woman confessed, and the Lord cleansed her; he showered her with his graciousness.

Pastor: Taste and see that the Lord is good; that blessings flow down upon those who take refuge in him. Whoever of you loves life and desires to see good in your days, keep your tongues from speaking lies; turn from evil and do good; seek peace and pursue it.

People: No one will be condemned who takes refuge in him. *(paraphrase of Psalm 34)*

Hymn: "We Praise Thee, O God, Our Redeemer" Kremser

Invocation and Lord's Prayer

*Alternate Praise Hymn: "Commune With Me" Kirk Dearman

*Alternate Hymn: "Have Thine Own Way, Lord!" Adelaide

Number 43

Pastor: "I appeal to you therefore, brothers and sisters, by the mercies of God, to present your bodies as a living sacrifice, holy and acceptable to God, which is your spiritual worship." *(Romans 12:1 NRSV)*

People: Present our bodies? What do our bodies have to do with our spirits?

Pastor: The Greeks asked the same thing of the apostle Paul. Paul, being a Jew, responded, "everything." Our bodies are the self-expressions of our spirits. What we believe about God, our neighbors, and ourselves, is demonstrated in our bodies.

People: The world tells us to indulge our bodies, pamper our bodies, aerobicize our bodies, give in to the lusts of our bodies. It tells us nothing about sacrificing our bodies to God.

Pastor: The light dawns! That's one reason we come to worship: to be reminded that we are whole beings, not compartmentalized segments. And with our whole beings we worship God in our work, in our play, in our interactions with others, and in the secret moments of our daily living. Every act of our lives is a statement about our faith in God.

People: *(To be sung)* "Take My Life, And Let It Be" Hendon "Take my life and let it be consecrated, Lord, to thee; take my hands and let them move, at the impulse of thy love, at the impulse of thy love.

"Take my feet and let them be, swift and beautiful for thee; take my voice and let me sing, always, only, for my King, always, only for my King."

Invocation and Lord's Prayer

Hymn of Celebration: "Ye Servants Of God, Your Master Proclaim" Hanover

73

Number 44

Pastor: Jesus says that there are many who have eyes but do not see; they have ears but do not hear.

People: That's hard to grasp. We have physical senses that were designed to inform us of the world around us. We are taking in information about people and things, moment by moment.

Pastor: But the truth is that we learn, early in life, to filter out many things that we are not interested in dealing with; and sin causes us to screen out many attempts by God to communicate with us. Therefore, we do have eyes but do not see the beckonings of God; we have ears but do not hear the call of God upon our lives to do his bidding.

People: Then, as we gather for worship, we must prepare ourselves by opening all of our senses to both his gentle pleadings and stern commands, that we may see life eternal, which he offers to those who can see his Son.

Hymn: *(copy in)* "Open Our Eyes, Lord"* Bob Cull

Pastor: This Jesus Christ: Whom does the world say that he is?

Women: Some say that he is a quaint and slightly irrelevant idealist.

Men: Some say that he is a great teacher of moral systems.

Women: Some say that he is a rebel, an anarchist, an iconoclast who seeks to destroy every precious tradition that has given life meaning for centuries.

Men: Some say that he is a dangerous man who must be destroyed, while others say that he is their only hope for a new beginning.

Pastor: Whom do you say that he is?

People: He is the Christ, the Son of the living God, the Redeemer of all who will claim his holy name!

Hymn: "All Hail The Power Of Jesus' Name"

Invocation and Lord's Prayer

Number 45

Pastor: Why have you come to church today; and what is happening in your life right now, that prepares you for your time with us?

People: We have come to worship, to renew friendships, to learn something new about the Lord, and ourselves, and to be forgiven for our sins. But whether we are ready for worship, we cannot say for sure.

Pastor: When young Isaiah was confronted by the Lord of Hosts, the holy God, in the sanctuary, he was immediately confronted by his sin: "Woe is me!" he cried out. He knew that he was a sinner in the midst of a people who were sinners. He knew that he must, as we must, be cleansed of his unrighteousness as he, and we, come before the Lord.

People: *(To be sung)* "Just As I Am" Woodworth
"Just as I am, without one plea, but that thy blood was shed for me; and that thou biddest me come to Thee — O Lamb of God, I come, I come!

"Just as I am, thy love unknown, hath broken every barrier down; now to be thine, yes, thine alone, O Lamb of God, I come, I come!"

Pastor: The apostle John promises us: "If we confess our sins, he is faithful and just, and will forgive our sins and cleanse us from all unrighteousness." *(1 John 1:9 RSV)* As we come to worship this morning, we must do so with a contrite heart, and a sense of openness, so that as we are emptied of our sins, we may be filled with the holy presence of God,

People: *(To be sung)* "Spirit Of The Living God" Living God
"Spirit of the Living God, fall afresh on me, Spirit of the Living God, fall afresh on me. Melt me, mold me, fill me, use me. Spirit of the Living God, fall afresh on me."

Number 46

Pastor: Choose!

People: We would rather keep our options open.

Pastor: Choose you this day!

People: We'd rather take some time to consider all of the possibilities.

Pastor: "I call heaven and earth to witness to you this day, that I have set before you life and death, blessing and curse; therefore choose life, that you and your descendents may live." *(Deuteronomy 30:19 RSV)*

People: Lord, that's strong language. But all important life choices have consequences which are heavily freighted. As we gather for worship, grant us the wisdom and the courage to choose life and holy blessing.

Hymn: "God of Grace and God of Glory" CWM Rhondda

Invocation and Lord's Prayer

Number 47

Pastor: We measure history by our wars, O God; and once more the armies are on the move. So once again, we gather together to worship, as men and women are dying.

People: With hearts filled with sadness over human failure to negotiate the peace, we seek your holy guidance in his hour. For you have called us to be your agents of peace, your proclaimers of righteousness, and your demonstrators of reconciliation.

Pastor: Teach us how to worship you so that our spirits will be strengthened.

People: Instruct us in your will so that we may fashion our lives in ways pleasing you.

Pastor: Give us guidance in how to pray,

People: That in a world filled with pain, we might be healers,

Pastor: That in a world entrapped in the tentacles of sin, your gracious power might bring release to those held captive,

People: That by the power of your Holy Spirit, we might be instruments of your peace. Amen.

Hymn: "Thou Whose Purpose Is To Kindle" Hyfrydol

Alternate Hymn: "O God, Our Help In Ages Past" St. Anne

Invocation and Lord's Prayer

Number 48

Pastor: As we come to worship:

Women: Focus us on your holy love;

Men: Center us on your just and righteous commandments;

Women: Direct us to your marvelous acts of mercy;

Men: Call us into obedience to your holy will,

Unison: That in this hour, your name might be glorified, and our lives might be redeemed.

Pastor: Holy, Holy, Holy! Lord God in highest heaven!

People: As the morning breaks upon us, our songs of praise rise up to thee.

Hymn: "Holy, Holy, Holy" Nicaea

Invocation And Lord's Prayer

Number 49

Pastor: The will of God!

People: The will of God?

Pastor: The will of God. In a few moments we will pray, "Thy will be done." We have come together to seek the will of God.

People: "Worthy art thou, our Lord and God, to receive glory and honor and power, for thou didst create all things, and by thy will they existed and were created." *(Revelation 4:11 RSV)*

People: *(To be sung) (copy in "Father I Believe You"* Sally Anderson)*

Pastor: But we must each one, be warned: surrendering to the will of God is not easy. Scripture warns us that the lust of the flesh and the eyes, and the pride of life in this world, shall entice us to destruction. To be victorious, we must rise above the evils of our day, and stand before the throne of God mature and fully assured in the will of God, in order that we may abide in his love forever.

People: *(To be sung) (copy in "I Surrender All" vv. 1, 2 Winfield Weeden)*

Invocation and Lord's Prayer

Hymn of Celebration: "Praise To The Lord, The Almighty" Lobe Den Herren

*Include CCLI Number

Number 50

Pastor: Most of our entry doors have two locks on them.

People: It's a dangerous world in which we live. We need to be careful.

Pastor: But the locked doors are not just on our homes and offices. Many of us have locked doors on our hearts, also.

People: It's a dangerous world in which we live. We need to be careful.

Pastor: And yet, the sad paradox is that in barring those who would injure us, we also often bar those who would heal us.

People: We yearn for friendship; we cry out for openness. And yet, where shall we start? Whom shall we trust?

Pastor: Jesus said, "Listen, I am standing at the door knocking; if you hear my voice and open the door, I will come in to you and eat with you, and you with me." *(Revelation 3:20 NRSV)*

People: *(To be sung) (copy in "Into My Heart"*)*

Pastor: Hear the great promise of scripture: "God is love, and those who abide in love abide in God, and God abides in them .... There is no fear in love, but perfect love casts out fear." *(1 John 4:16, 18 NRSV)* Come to worship the God of love, enter into his holy presence with thanksgiving in your hearts for the unsearchable riches of joy, peace, security, and holy affection which you shall receive at the throne of grace.

Hymn: "The Wonder Of It All" George Beverly Shea

Invocation and Lord's Prayer

*Include CCLI Number

6 — Seasonal Calls To Worship

Number 51
The New Year

Pastor: We mark our days and measure our lives by the years. But to the eternal God, all generations are equal and their passing is an everpresent moment.

People: We say, "I was," "I am," "I will be."

Pastor: God says, "I am that I am. My name is 'Eternal Present.'"

People: We struggle to live 70 years, maybe 80, perhaps even 90 or 100 years, and hope that we may live bravely in the process — and make some small difference for a lifetime of efforts.

Pastor: Be assured: Whatever is done in the name of the Lord, that deed will last for eternity.

People: We receive this new year, and acknowledge that it's a priceless gift from the Lord. As we come to worship, we give that gift back to our God, with our commitment to live with him or to die with him, but always to share in the victory with him, for all the years that he shall grant to us on this earth.

Pastor: Remember the psalmist's affirmation: "All the days ordained for me were written in your book before one of them came to be." *(Psalm 139:16 NIV)*

People: We claim it as our own. O God, as we come together to worship you for the first time this year, grant that we may use those new days as opportunities to accomplish that which is pleasing in your sight, and make us sources of spiritual beauty to those who depend upon us for a word from you. Amen.

Hymn: "O God, Our Help In Ages Past" St. Anne

Pastor: Jesus Christ is the Alpha and the Omega. The beginning and the end. He was with God from before the beginning; and he is seated at the right hand of God to receive us at the end. The God of our mothers led them in the paths of righteousness; the God of our fathers granted goodness and mercy to them on their journeys. In these latter days this same God, through his Son Jesus Christ, shall lead us forth on the roads of right living with his merciful hand.

People: Praise be to God, whose divine love shall rule the living of our days.

Invocation and Lord's Prayer

Hymn Of Celebration: "How Great Thou Art" Stuart K. Hine

Number 52

Pastor: Hear the words of the apostle Paul: "May the God of steadfastness and encouragement grant you to live in such harmony with one another in accord with Christ Jesus, that together you may with one voice, glorify the God and Father of our Lord Jesus Christ." *(Romans 15:5-6 RSV)*

People: *(To be sung) (copy in "The Bond Of Love"* Bond Of Love)*

Pastor: But how do we say that we are one, when diversity and dis-unity are the features of human living upon which we are most focused, day after day? After all, we may be Native American, European, Asian, African,

People: We may be female or male,

Pastor: We may be economically deprived or wealthy,

People: We may belong to professional societies or to the laboring force,

Pastor: We may be dark-skinned or light, multi-talented or blessed with one skill ...

People: But in Jesus Christ we are one people, in God the Father we are sisters and brothers in the Lord, and in the Holy Spirit we come to worship and fellowship under the one name whereby we might be saved.

Hymn: "The Church's One Foundation" Aurelia

Invocation and Lord's Prayer

Medley of Praise
　　"Bind Us Together" Bob Gillman
　　"Jesus Is Lord Of All" William Gaither
　　"He Is Lord" He Is Lord

*Include CCLI Number

Number 53
Scout Sunday

Pastor: "I promise to love God . . . ." "I promise to do my best to do my duty to God . . . ." Those are hard promises to keep.

People: In fact, they are promises that are beyond our ability to keep, unless we pray for God to help us in that pledge.

Pastor: "On my honor . . . ." "I believe that America's strength lies in her trust in God . . . ." Honor, trust, courage, and duty are hard words,

People: But necessary to emulate, if we are to build a strong community and live lives pleasing to God.

Pastor: As young people and old, we come together to praise God, to give thanks for leaders who have directed us and inspired us in the past, and for a future that calls out of each young person, the very best that we have to offer to God.

People: As we gather for worship, we are reminded that we are surrounded by a great cloud of witnesses who have gone before us, set us an example for dedicated living, and lovingly yearn for that day when, in heaven, we may join our voices together in praising the God of gods, the Lord of lords, and King of kings.

Hymn: "For All The Saints" Sine Nomine

Invocation and Lord's Prayer

Greeting:

Pastor: Who is this?

People: Who is this who comes?

Pastor: Who is this who comes riding on a donkey?

People: Who is this who comes riding on a colt, the foal of a donkey?

Unison: *(To be sung)* "All Glory, Laud, and Honor" v. 1 St. Theodulph
"All glory, laud, and honor to thee, Redeemer, King, to whom the lips of children made sweet hosannas ring: thou art the King of Israel, thou David's royal Son, who in the Lord's name comest, the King and blessed one!"

Pastor: This is the King!

People: This is the King, the Son of David, the Son of Man!

Pastor: This is the Blessed One, who comes in the name of the Lord!

People: This is the Son of Man for whom angels have prepared the way!

Pastor: This is the Son of God, who causes the angelic choruses to sing, "Hosanna in the highest!"

Unison: *(To be sung)* "All Glory, Laud, And Honor" v. 2
"The company of angels are praising thee on high, and mortal men and all things created make reply: the people of the Hebrews with palms before thee went; our praise and prayer and anthems before thee we present."

Pastor: Come, you who would worship him. Prepare his path, make straight his way. Lay before him your garments, that his pilgrimage may be evident to all who pass this way.

(over)   87

People: Blessed is he who brings us his salvation. For this is Jesus of Nazareth, the Son of God sent from heaven to earth, that we might be redeemed!

Unison: *(To be sung)* "All Glory, Laud, And Honor" v. 3. "To thee, before thy passion, they sang their hymns of praise; to thee, now high exalted, our melody we raise: thou didst accept their praises — accept the praise we bring, who in all good delightest, thou good and gracious King!"

Invocation and Lord's Prayer

Hymn of Celebration: "Crown Him With Many Crowns" Diademata

Number 55
Palm Sunday

Pastor: It's a parade!

People: A what?

Pastor: A parade! A celebration! A moment in time when the people must shout and sing:

People: Hosanna! Glory to the Son, and to the God who granted him to us!

Pastor: For he has come into our midst to save his people!

People: Gather branches from the trees! Lay your coats in his path! Make ready the way of our Savior! Prepare the path for the Lord!

Pastor: Come before him in worship. Prepare your hearts to receive the King of kings.

People: *(To be sung) (copy in "All Hail King Jesus"* Dave Moody)*

Invocation and Lord's Prayer

Hymn of Celebration: "Lift Up Your Heads, Ye Mighty Gates"

*Include CCLI Number

Number 56
Easter Sunday

Pastor: Imagine the darkness. The darkness that comes before the dawn, of course. But think about the darkness of the soul — when all hope is apparently lost, when any possibility of victory has been denied, when death puts an end to the dreams of life that dwell deep in the human heart.

People: *(To be sung)* **"Low in the grave he lay, Jesus, my Savior! Waiting the coming day, Jesus, my Lord!"***

Pastor: The miracles. The healings. The compassionate touch. The words of condemnation and reassurance. The teachings about God, who loves us more deeply than the most devoted parent. Gone! Dead! Sealed in a tomb!

People: *(To be sung)* **"Vainly they watched his bed, Jesus, my Savior! Vainly they sealed the dead, Jesus, my Lord!"**

Pastor: How foolish was Pilate, preening himself in his puny power. How myopic were the members of the Sanhedrin, supposing a simple solution would seal the fate of their adversary: the Son of God! The Savior of humanity!

People: *(To be sung)* **"Death could not keep his prey, Jesus, my Savior! He tore the bars away, Jesus, my Lord!"**

Pastor: Come ye then! Gather to worship with praise and proclamation on your lips! For the worst that sinful humanity could accomplish, has been overcome by the best that divine love could accomplish!

People: *(To be sung)* **"Up from the grave he arose, with a mighty triumph o'er his foes; he arose a victor from the dark domain, and he lives forever with his saints to reign; He arose! He arose! Hallelujah! Christ Arose!"**

Invocation and Lord's Prayer

Hymn of Celebration: "Jesus Christ Is Risen Today" Llanfair

*"**Christ Arose"** Robert Lowry

90

Number 57
Easter Sunday

Pastor: Secret places!

People: Secret places?

Pastor: Secret places! God does some of his most fascinating work in the secret places. He knit us together in the secret place of the womb, fashioning us and shaping us for life on this earth. Secretly, in the darkness just before the dawn, he overcame sin and death, raising to life, his Son who had been put to death upon the cross in order that we might have eternal life in him.

People: "Praise God, from whom all blessings flow."

Pastor: But the most secret place of all is the secret chamber of the heart: that place in men and women, where dwells, the most private of our thoughts and yearnings. Our true identity lies amongst our secrets. In order that we may claim the resurrection as our own, our hearts must be opened before the Lord as fully as the angel opened the tomb of our risen Savior on the first Easter morn.

People: Almighty God, there is no heart that can be sealed off from you, who know all of our desires and yearnings, all of our plans and secrets. Cleanse our hearts and our minds, redeem our thoughts and our schemes through the indwelling of your Holy Spirit, in order that we may more perfectly love you, and more worthily magnify your holy name; through Christ our risen Lord. Amen.

Pastor: Now are we truly ready to give praise to the Lord of lords, on this day of days.

Hymn: "Thine Is The Glory" Judas Maccabeus

Invocation and Lord's Prayer

Number 58
Memorial Sunday

Pastor: Lord, you have been our dwelling place in all generations

People: Before the mountains were brought forth, before you had formed the earth and granted it the first rays of light, you are from everlasting to everlasting.

Pastor: You are the God of our fathers, and the Lord who has given guidance to our mothers.

People: In their joys and sorrows, they lifted their voices unto you, and you heard them and ministered to them. Blessed is your name, O Holy One to be praised!

Pastor: As you were present in the '90s and 1090s, and 1890s, be present with us in the 1990s so that we may join our voices to a mighty chorus of praise and thanksgiving through the centuries.

People: And give us a vision for the future that gives honor to the past. For you are our God yesterday, today, tomorrow, and forevermore.

Hymn: "For All The Saints" Sine Nomine

Invocation and Lord's Prayer

Number 59
Memorial Sunday

Pastor: I am.

People: Who?

Pastor: I am the God of your fathers.

People: Who are you, Lord?

Pastor: I am the God of your mothers and fathers, grandparents and great grandparents.

People: What?

Pastor: I am the God who created the earth and established my nation, Israel.

People: What have you to do with us?

Pastor: I am the God of your history, your heritage, who, in the fullness of time, sent my Son, that those who believe in him might have eternal life.

People: Why?

Pastor: I am the God who was, and is, and always shall be faithful to the children of every generation.

People: Why have you visited us with your holy presence?

Pastor: As I have offered salvation and life eternal to your kinfolks of an earlier day, so now do I call you to repentance.

People: Where?

Pastor: As I have called your mothers and fathers to faithfulness and commitment, I now call you to lives of devotion to me.

People: Where shall we worship you?

Pastor: You shall worship me in the high places and the low, in season and out of season; you shall worship me in my house and bring your praises before the throne of grace.

People: "I was glad when they said to me, 'Let us go to the house of the Lord!' " "Enter his gates with thanksgiving and his courts with praise! Give thanks to him and bless his holy name." "For the Lord is good; his steadfast love endures throughout the years, and his faithfulness is as secure in this generation as in every generation past." *(Psalm 122:1, 100:4-5 RSV)*

Hymn: "God Of Our Fathers" National Hymn

Invocation and Lord's Prayer

Number 60
Pentecost Sunday

Pastor: It was a day like any other, and a day like no other. They had gathered themselves in one place. What was to happen next? They could not imagine. And then a great sound — a heavenly sound — filled the room where they sat. It was like a mighty wind, but the dust went undisturbed. And then there were tongues. Were they composed of fire? They rested upon each of them and they were filled with the Holy Spirit, and they began speaking to one another in tongues, as they were guided by the Spirit.

People: *(To be sung) (copy in "Glorify Thy Name"* Donna Adkins) (use "Spirit" in place of "Father")*

Pastor: Who can control the wind? We hear the sound of it and we see the effects of its passing. But we neither give it direction, nor do we put an end to its movement. So it is with the Spirit. It enters into women and men who are prepared to open their lives to the Holy One of God.

People: *(To be sung) (copy in "Glorify Thy Name," same as above)*

Pastor: Jesus said, "If you love me, you will keep my commandments." *(John 14:15)* And he tells us that the Father will give us a Holy Spirit, the Spirit of Truth, a Counselor and Comforter, who will dwell with us and in us.

People: *(To be sung) (copy in "Glorify Thy Name" using "Father")*

Pastor: It is in the Holy Spirit that we have life; for God, who raised his Son Jesus Christ from the dead, gives life to our fleshly beings through his Spirit which dwells in us. In the Spirit of God we have daily guidance and an advocate before the throne of grace: As we read in scripture, "Likewise, the Spirit helps us in our weakness; for we do not know how to pray

95

as we ought, but the Spirit himself intercedes for us with sighs too deep for words." *(Romans 8:26 RSV)* Therefore, as we come together to worship, we have the assurance that the Spirit, who knows the will of God, will himself lead us in worshiping God.

People: *(To be sung) (copy in "Glorify Thy Name" using "Spirit")*

Invocation and Lord's Prayer

Hymn of Celebration: "Sweet, Sweet, Spirit" Doris Akers

*Include CCLI Number

Number 61
Independence Day

Pastor: You have granted us a land, O God.

People: A land abundantly filled with minerals and vegetables, fields and forests, and mountains and rivers.

Pastor: You have granted us a heritage, O God.

People: A government of the people, with legislatures and courts, assembly halls and schools, and due process and social institutions.

Pastor: You have granted us labor and productivity, O Lord.

People: Industries and shops, foundries and labs, libraries, homes and mills, where we may grow and produce, create and design, and honor you and serve our neighbors through our ingenuity and labor.

Pastor: You have granted us the freedom of worship, O God.

People: So that we may give thanks to you for your loving kindness, and praise you for the bounty which you have provided, and humble ourselves before you in our sinfulness, so that we may be forgiven and set free to serve you forever.

Pastor: In our worship this day, may we be reminded of our pleasure in being sons of God.

People: In our adoration this day, may we be strengthened in our faithfulness as daughters of the Most High.

Hymn: "My Country 'Tis Of Thee" Henry Carey

Invocation and Lord's Prayer

Number 62
Independence Day

Hymn: "America The Beautiful" (vv. 1-2)

Litany Of Citizenship

Pastor: We are citizens of two commonwealths: the kingdom of God and the kingdom of Man.

People: O Lord, it's hard to clarify our responsibilities to each and to maintain our allegiances in their proper perspective.

Pastor: As citizens of the human kingdom, we have responsibilities to our own community, as well as to the community of nations. As Jesus put it, "You are the salt of the earth;" and again, "Go and make disciples of all nations, baptizing them in the name of the Father and of the Son and of the Holy Spirit, teaching them to obey everything I have commanded you." *(Matthew 28:20)*

People: As citizens of the human kingdom, it is our task to:
1. **Be defenders of religious liberty,**
2. **Provide asylum for the persecuted,**
3. **Protect the children from ignorance, want, and abuse,**
4. **Make available to all citizens the right to pursue those goals which are not destructive to human life and welfare.**
5. **And participate in the governance of the people for the good of all who reside within our borders.**

Pastor: As citizens of the kingdom of God, we have responsibilities to our Creator and Savior.

People: We come this morning to:
1. **Give thanks for our earthly lives and our eternal salvation,**
2. **Seek guidance in living lives that demonstrate moral purity,**

98

3. Ask forgiveness for our sinful ways,
4. Bring our petitions of healing and mercy on behalf of those who suffer,
5. And pray for our nation to preserve spiritual freedom and our government to seek your guidance in making decisions that affect the daily lives of your children.

Unison: Above all, we acknowledge you as Lord of lords, our God who is above all principalities and powers, to whom we give all honor and praise today, tomorrow, and forevermore.

Hymn: "America The Beautiful" (vv. 3-4)

Invocation and Lord's Prayer

Number 63
Advent Sundays

First Sunday: Lighting the Advent wreath and proclaiming the gospel

Reader: In the beginning, God created the heavens and the earth. The earth was without form and void, and darkness was upon the face of the deep. And God said, "Let there be light;" and there was light. *(Genesis 1:3)*

People: This is the message we have heard from him and declare to you: "God is light; and in him there is no darkness at all." *(1 John 1:5)*

Reader: Darkness covered the hearts and minds of men and women, also. The children were born into spiritual darkness.

People: Jesus said, "I am the light of the world; he who follows me will not walk in darkness, but will have the light of life." *(John 8:12)*

Reader: As we light the first candle of Advent, we remember the promise of the apostle John: "The light shines in the darkness and the darkness has not overcome it." *(John 1:5)*

Reader: Dear God, as you promised light and life to the ancient peoples of the Roman world, rekindle that promise within our hearts today. For we also live in a world where darkness often reigns. You are our lamp, O Lord; turn our darkness into light. Amen.

Hymn: "Let All Mortal Flesh Keep Silent" Picardy

Pastor: "The people who sat in darkness have seen a great light, and for those who sat in the region and shadow of death, light has dawned." *(Matthew 4:16)*

People: We are a chosen race, a royal priesthood, God's own people, that we may declare the wonderful deeds of him who called us out of darkness into his marvelous light. Once we were no people; but now we are God's people." *(1 Peter 2:9)*

Pastor: What you are told in the dark, utter in the light; and what you hear whispered, proclaim upon the housetops!'' *(Matthew 10:27)*

Invocation and Lord's Prayer

Hymn of Celebration: ''As With Gladness Men Of Old'' Dix

Number 64

Second Sunday: Lighting the Advent wreath and proclaiming the gospel

Reader: Advent means a coming. It's a time of joyful expectation, a time of quiet waiting for the coming one.

People: In the midst of stress-filled days, over-loaded calendars, crowded stores, and anxiety over loneliness or family estrangement during the holiday season, help us to experience moments of quiet waiting, O Lord; and grant us the gift of joy-filled expectation of the re-birth of love within our hearts.

Reader: The Advent wreath grew out of a pagan German custom to celebrate the winter solstice. This fire ring was connected to the worship of the sun. It represented revelry, over-indulgence, and suicide. The Christians took the popular fire ring and redeemed it, cleansed it, and gave it new meaning, symbolizing the preparation for the birth of Christ.

People: We too have lived lives displeasing to God, and more focused upon destruction than upon life. As you have redeemed the pagan symbols of old, and infused them with the representation of the true light, redeem our lives today, O God, and bring your healing light to the dark corners of our souls.

Reader: Today this wreath represents the cycle of thousands of years from Adam to Christ, during which the world awaited the coming of a redeemer. And now it also represents the cycle of years when the word awaits the second Advent, the second coming of our Lord.

People: Expectancy and hope! Priceless gifts that the world seldom offers. Renew our lives this day, O God, grant us these gifts wherever we are on life's journey, that we may be refreshed.

Reader: As we light the second candle, hear the words of Isaiah: "Seek the Lord while he may be found; call on him while he is near. Let the wicked forsake their way and the unrighteous their thoughts; let them return to the Lord, that he may have mercy on them, and to our God, for he will abundantly pardon .... You shall go out in joy and be led back in peace; the mountains and the hills before you shall burst into song and all the trees of the field shall clap their hands." *(Isaiah 55:6-7, 12 NRSV)*

Hymn: "Come, Thou Long-Expected Jesus" Hyfrydol

Pastor: Hear the word of the Lord: "As the rain and the snow come down from heaven, and do not return to it without watering the earth and making it bud and flourish, so that it yields seed for the sower and bread for the eater, so it is my word that goes out from my mouth:

People: "It will not return to me empty, but will accomplish what I desire and achieve the purpose for which I sent it." *(Isaiah 55:10-11 RSV)*

Pastor: As you come together to worship today, receive the seed of the Word, that God may accomplish in you, that good purpose for which it is sent.

Invocation and Lord's Prayer

Hymn of Celebration: "O Come, O Come, Emmanuel" Veni Emmanuel

Number 65

Third Sunday: Lighting the Advent wreath and proclaiming the gospel

Reader: They were unremarkable men, of little note in their community. Their names go unrecorded in history.

People: And yet, they were first to receive the good news. The great news! The astounding news!

Reader: The sky was dark, the towns and villages were quiet. The sun had long since vacated the sky. The shepherds were drowsy, and quietly exchanged the last stories of the day.

People: Who could have dreamed of such an event? Whose imagination could have prepared them for this honor? What prophet's voice would have convinced these shepherds that their lives would be so blessed?

Reader: And yet, the darkness was shattered. The night sky was torn in two. "An angel of the Lord appeared to them, and the glory of the Lord shone around them, and they were filled with fear." *(Luke 2:9)*

People: These common men received the revelation of God Almighty, proclaimed by the angel: "Behold, I bring you good news of great joy, which will come to all people: for to you is born in the city of David, a Savior, who is Christ the Lord." *(Luke 2:11)*

Reader: Today we light the third candle of Advent which commemorates the shepherds: humble men whose hearts were open to receiving God's revelation.

Let us pray: O God, we need not be princesses or presidents to receive the great good news of your saving act for all peoples. All we need is to be open to your spirit, that we might receive your revelations. We open our hearts to you, that you might speak to us as you did to the women and men of old. Amen.

Hymn: "While Shepherds Watch Their Flock By Night"
Christmas

Pastor: "Gloria in excelsis Deo!" cried the multitude of angels who filled the skies with their praises of God that night.

People: If even the angels must worship God and sing his praises, how can we do less, as we gather in the name of his Son, whose birth we anticipate this holy season?

Pastor: The wilderness shall rejoice; the desert shall blossom. The people of earth shall see the glory of the Lord, and the majesty of our God. Weak hands shall be strengthened and frail legs shall be made strong. Then the eyes of the blind shall be opened;

People: The ears of the deaf unstopped,

Pastor: The lame shall leap like the deer,

People: And the tongues of the speechless shall sing for joy.

Pastor: A highway shall be there, and it shall be called the Holy Way; and the ransomed of the Lord shall come to Zion with singing. Sorrow and grief shall flee away before the gladness of God. Grief and despair shall be overwhelmed by God's glory. *(Isaiah 35)*

Invocation and the Lord's Prayer

Hymn of Celebration: "Angels We Have Heard On High"
Gloria

Number 66

Fourth Sunday: Lighting the Advent wreath and proclaiming the gospel

Reader: Jesus said that there will be signs in the heavens, and distress among the nations of earth. The earth and the sea shall be shaken; and the powers of heaven will be stirred up. Then shall we see the Son of Man returning to earth with power and great glory. He tells us that when these things happen, we can be certain that our redemption is drawing near.

People: As we live with hope in the second coming, our minds turn today, to the first coming of the Lord.

Reader: As Jesus prophesied his return, so Isaiah prophecied that first time of his dwelling with us: "In that day the root of Jesse shall stand as a banner for the peoples; him shall the nations seek, and his dwellings shall be glorious." *(Isaiah 11:10)* He came out of love; he came to reconcile us to himself; he came to give us peace in the midst of turmoil; he came to bring healing to the injured and to those who are mortally wounded in their souls.

People: We give praise to the Lord who redeems us, to the God of our salvation.

Reader: As we light the fourth candle of Advent, we remember the holy gifts promised to us through the psalmist: "By day the Lord commands his steadfast love; and at night his song is with me, a prayer to the God of my life." *(Psalm 42:8 RSV)* Love by day; a song to carry us through the night. These are gifts beyond price.

People: Great is the Lord, and greatly to be praised! As we gather in worship, our eyes behold the flame; and once more, we celebrate the birth of Immanuel, the Christ, who shall dwell with us through all generations.

Reader: Let us pray: O Lord, you have brought light to our dark souls, even as you have brought brightness to our eyes.

"The great day of the Lord is near, and hastening fast." *(Zephaniah 1:14 RSV)* Prepare our hearts to receive you, that through your grace, we may be found worthy to be received by you into your holy kingdom forevermore. Amen.

Hymn: "Hark The Herald Angels Sing" Mendelssohn

Pastor: As we look forward to "The Coming," and back to "The Coming," we are reminded of the prophecy of Zechariah concerning his son John: "Praise be to the Lord, the God of Israel, because he has come to redeem his people .... And you, my child, shall prepare the way for the Lord, to give to his people the knowledge of salvation through the forgiveness of their sins through the tender mercy of our God, when the day shall dawn upon us from on high to give light to those who sit in darkness and in the shadow of death, to guide our feet in the way of peace. *(Luke 1:86ff RSV)*

Invocation and Lord's Prayer

Hymn of Celebration: "Joy To The World" Antioch

7 — Preparations For Pastoral Prayer

Number 67

Prepare a card that can be taken home for personal devotions, after use in worship. Design it as follows:

Mark 10:35-37, 47-51

Jesus: "What do you want me to do for you?"

James & John; "Make us important."

Blind Bartimaeus: "Let me receive my sight."

Me:_____

Devotional Thought For The Congregation:

As we come together in prayers of praise and petition, it's good for us to examine our expectations and requests. Mark 10 tells how Jesus twice asked his petitioners, "What do you want me to do for you?" His disciples petitioned him in self-centered arrogance. Bartimaeus reached out in faith to the only hope available to release him from his disability. As you come before the Lord this morning, what is your most important petition? Ask the Holy Spirit to help you select one, and write it on your card. In a few moments, we will come before the Lord with our requests.

Sing a devotional hymn

Pastoral Prayer

Number 68

Copy into the bulletin, Romans 15:13 (NIV): "May the God of hope fill you with all joy and peace as you trust in him, so that you may overflow with hope by the power of the Holy Spirit."

Devotional Thought For The Congregation:
Most of the time, our prayer requests seem to center on physical diseases and material requests. Though these are legitimate parts of prayer, there is so much more to our communication with God to which we could avail ourselves. Consider the scripture verse in the bulletin. Notice the many powerful, imaginative, creative words in that one passage: "hope," "joy," "peace," "trust," "overflow," and "power." As we move into a time of prayer, I encourage you to select one of these words that is meaningful to you in this moment, and with the guidance of the Holy Spirit, reflect upon the significance of that word for you today.

Quiet music, or appropriate hymn

Pastoral Prayer

Number 69

Copy in the words to "Teach Us What We Yet May Be," Ode To Joy, words by Catherine Arnott. (Include your CCLI Number) Underline the phrases, "share inventive powers," "teach us what we yet may be," "we have conquered," "known the ecstasy," "probed the secrets of the atom," "children of creative purpose," "dreams rich with meaning," and "our work is one." Then include in the bulletin:

Points To Ponder:
1. We are partners with God in his creative enterprise.
2. We are inventors, conquerors, dreamers, probers, workers.
3. As "children of creative power," how should we come to the Lord in prayer today?
4. What are we willing to risk, if we're willing to pray, "Teach us what we yet may be?"

Devotional Thoughts For The Congregation
Often we come to God in our weakness:
I'm old Lord — sick Lord — a sinner
My future has passed Lord — I'm unable to act Lord
Today we come to God in our strength
We have talents and skills, Lord
We have life and relationships, Lord
We have wisdom, insight, resources

As we enter into prayer, let's do so with the question, how can we be more effective partners with God in the enterprise of life?

Pastoral Prayer

Number 70

Devotional Thought For The Congregation:
As we enter into our prayer time, let's think about love. There are all kinds of love: love that "does for," and love that "stands back." There is soft love and tough love, mushy love and confronting love. As you reflect upon where you are in your journey right now, consider the question, "how can God's love best serve me today?"

Prayer Hymn
A medley of:
"I Love You Lord" Laurie Klein
"We Are So Blessed" William Gaither and Greg Nelson
Alternate Hymn
"Day By Day" Blott En Dag

Pastoral Prayer

Number 71

**Devotional Thought For The Congregation
(Advent/Christmas):**

The author served as a pastor in Eastern Idaho when the Teton Dam gave way, flooding many cities, towns, and farms. Volunteers went into the flood area to help residents clean up. Our crew went to the farm community of Roberts. The five-foot wall of water had passed through an oil tank farm and a cattle feed lot before going through homes and yards. The water was highly polluted and contaminated everything. Volunteers were told to enter the area, wearing clothing that could be put in plastic bags and later burned, after working in the area. I felt peculiar, and estranged from the people whom we were helping, because we stripped ourselves of the contaminants when we left; but they had to continue living in the harmful pollution after we were gone. They could not go home to safety and clean living, like we could. They could not burn their clothes and be quit of the place, like we could.

In many charitable activities, we take care of the hungry, homeless, hurting, dispossessed, imprisoned, offering them a variety of services, and then we go back to the safety of our well-stocked homes. That's the best that most humans can do.

But Jesus jumps into the roiling waters with us; he slogs through the mud with us. He embraces us, and in the process, gets the dirt of our sin on himself. "Christ Jesus, who, though he was in the form of God, did not count equality with God as something to be exploited, but emptied himself, taking the form of a slave, being born in human likeness. And being found in human form, he humbled himself and became obedient to the point of death — even death on a cross." *(Philippians 2:6-8 NRSV)*

That's the story of Christmas. As we enter into a time of prayer, let us consider how Jesus entered into our world at its crudest point. "What child is this, who, laid to rest, on Mary's lap is sleeping? Why lies he in such mean estate, where ox and ass were feeding? This is Christ the King, whom shepherds guard and angels sing.''

He joined our mean estate, that one day we might join his exalted estate.

Prayer Hymn: "What Child Is This, Who, Laid To Rest?" Greensleeves

Pastoral Prayer

Number 72

Devotional Thoughts For The Congregation:
As we enter into a time of prayer, I want us to think about names. Names have meanings: David means "beloved." Michael means "Angel of God." Linda means "pretty." George means "farmer." *(List other appropriate names, meaningful to the setting)* In the past, people often named people for spiritual qualities, such as faith, hope, and grace.

God and Jesus both changed peoples' names to indicate a new relationship: Jacob became Israel — "struggler with God," Cephus became Peter — "the rock." As you come before God in prayer this morning, what name would you like from God? Might it be: faithful — trustworthy — redeemed? My witness — patient one — strong in the Lord? Let's ask God about our names today.

Prayer Medley
"Jesus, Name Above All Names" Naida Hearn
"His Name Is Wonderful" Mieir

Pastoral Prayer

Devotional Thought For The Congregation:
Our faces take on the image of our environments.
1. Some say that pets and their owners look alike.
2. Others say that husbands and wives acquire the same expressions.

Our faces tell many stories — they betray what's happening inside our lives, particularly to those who know how to read us.
1. People who lead hard lives, angry lives, take on a hard, angry look.
2. People who spend much time in the holy places of God seem to develop an aura around their faces, radiating a gentle spirit and a sense of peace and hope that comes from dwelling in the presence of God.

The Bible talks about this:
1. Deuteronomy 34:29: "When Moses ... came down from the mountain, he did not know that the skin of his face shone because he had been talking to God."
2. Psalm 34:5: "Look to him and be radiant; so your faces shall never be ashamed."

As we enter into prayer time, I encourage you to think about what your face reflects, and to think about what effect your countenance has upon other people for good or for ill.

Prayer Medley
"Let The Beauty Of Jesus Be Seen In Me"
"Altogether Lovely"
"Something Beautiful"
"Breathe On Me, Breath Of God" vv. 1, 3

Number 74

Devotional Thought For The Congregation:
How do we come to the Lord at a time of prayer?
1. Some come, in charge.
   a. "Lord, here's the problem and here's what you need to do."
   b. Some come with no idea that personal preparation is necessary for effective prayer.
2. To be effective, we must first empty ourselves of self.

Hymn: "I Surrender All," vv. 1, 4 Surrender

Entering into the sanctuary of God:
1. Only as we're emptied of self can we enter fully into the presence of God.
2. Here our focus is totally on him, not self — on his holiness, compassion, sense of just, righteousness, mercy.
3. Contemplating these things, now how, and for what, do we ask?

Hymn: "Near To The Heart Of God" vv. 1, 2 McAfee

Now we're ready to reconsider ourselves — not in relation to our own wants and preconceptions, but as we stand in contrast to the Lord:
1. One thing we see is that what others should first see in us is not our own cleverness, magnificence, beauty — but rather the beauty of Jesus, shining through.
2. Once this happens, then our own best talents/skills shine through, polished by the richness of a holy presence in our lives.
3. Now we truly want what God wants for our concerns, and for our loved ones.

Hymn: "Let The Beauty Of Jesus Be Seen In Me"

Pastoral Prayer

Hymn: "Things Are Different Now" Stanton Gavitt

Alternate Hymn: "Since Jesus Came Into My Heart" McDaniel

Number 75

Devotional Thought For The Congregation:

Praise Hymn: "Behold What Manner Of Love" Patricia Van Tine

There's a rollicking, lilting tune: We can almost see clowns dancing up on the chancel.
1. Maybe not clowns, but fools — fools for God.
2. As we prepare for prayer, think about being a fool for God.

(2 Corinthians 11:16ff) The apostle Paul — If we think of him as foolish, he'll gladly be a fool for the Lord.
1. Many people make themselves fools for other things:
    a. Fame — what foolish things people do in public for notoriety.
    b. Politics — what foolish things people do/say to get votes.
    c. Power — what fools we are to give away things most precious to us (family, integrity, honorable name), to gain power.
    d. Independence — what fools we be to destroy loving relationships and physical/mental health, to show that we are independent.
2. Paul will be a fool for God, to receive the love of God:
    a. Boasting in his weakness, that he might glory in the strength of the Lord.
    b. Boasting in his suffering, that through his life, others might find salvation.

Allowing ourselves to be thought a fool strips us of our dignity and personal stature, taking a heavy toll on our pride.
1. Only then can God use us in that capacity which he intended for us.
2. In this prayer time, let's deal with foolishness and pride — and being a fool for God.

Pastoral Prayer

Praise Hymn: "To God Be The Glory" My Tribute

Number 76

Prayer And Praise

Hymn: *(copy in "Christ, We Do All Adore Thee" Adore Thee)*

Reasons For Praise From The Letter To The Hebrews:

Pastor: "We see Jesus, who for a little while was made lower than the angels, now crowned with glory and honor because of the suffering of death, so that by the grace of God he might taste death for everyone." *(2:9)*

People: "Because he himself was tested by what he suffered, he is able to help those who are being tested." *(2:18)*

Pastor: "For we do not have a high priest who is unable to sympathize with our weaknesses, but we have one who in every respect has been tested as we are, yet without sin. Let us therefore approach the throne of grace with boldness, so that we may receive mercy and find grace to help in time of need. *(4:15-16)*

People: "And just as it is appointed for mortals to die once, and after that the judgment, so Christ, having been offered once to bear the sins of many, will appear a second time, not to deal with sin, but to save those who are eagerly waiting for him." *(9:27-28)*

Pastor: "Therefore, since we are surrounded by so great a cloud of witnesses, let us also lay aside every weight of sin that clings so closely, and let us run with perseverance the race that is set before us, looking to Jesus the pioneer and perfecter of our faith." *(12:1-2) (all NRSV)*

Hymn: *(copy in "What Wondrous Love Is This" Wondrous Love)*

Pastoral Prayer

Number 77

Preparation For Prayer:

(Copy into the bulletin) As you enter into prayer today, you may want to ask for a gift. It may be for a material thing, an experience, a spiritual blessing, a strengthening or healing, a new opportunity. If God were to grant that gift to you, how would you use it? To what advantage, and to whose advantage? And if God grants you a gift today, would you be willing to grant someone else a gift? What might that be?

Prayer Hymn: "It Is No Secret" Stuart Hamblen

Pastoral Prayer

Number 78

Devotional Thought For The Congregation:

The longest journey in life is from Palm Sunday to Easter Sunday — from a shallow celebration to a celebration coming from the depths of life and exploding into eternity.

1. Folks on the first Palm Sunday were happy to get on board a success train.
   a. Glad to rally around the flag.
      1. Go with the popular crowd.
      2. We like being on a winning team.
   b. Who'd pass up a chance to celebrate God's gift of a Messiah who'd give them a better life?
2. But when the going got tough, they melted away like wax figures on a hot July sidewalk.
   a. Only those who went with him through the cross and the resurrection, could find the true victory.
   b. Only those who committed their lives, could find salvation.
3. As we sing our prayer hymn, "Where He Leads Me," we're only going to sing two verses, which will leave us in the garden where we must make choices, just as Jesus had to make a crucial choice.
4. Our basic life choices are no less crucial.
   a. Whose will will you serve?
   b. Yours, or the Lord's?

Hymn: "Where He Leads Me" Norris

"I can hear my Savior calling, I can hear my Savior calling, I can hear my Savior calling, 'Take thy cross and follow, follow me.' "

Refrain: "Where he leads me I will follow, where he leads me I will follow, where he leads me I will follow, I'll go with him, with him, all the way.

"I'll go with him through the garden, I'll go with him through the garden, I'll go with him through the garden, I'll go with him, with him, all the way."

Pastoral Prayer

Number 79

Devotional Thought For The Congregation:

1. Think of some items in your life that remind you of your connections.
    a. A tool, a kitchen utensil, some crocheting, a painting that reminds you of a parent or grandparent.
    b. Maybe it's a place: the old neighborhood, a house, a vacation spot, or a theater, that reminds you of a relationship with family.
2. On Memorial Day weekend, you need to remember how we're connected to the past.
    a. For connections give us our identity.
    b. They give us a name and meaning for our existence.
    c. One of the devastating experiences of being homeless, or a refugee in the world, is to be disconnected.
        1. A person without connections loses his importance to the community — and to history.
        2. As we enter into prayer, giving thanks for our connectedness, we need to pray for those who have lost their connections.
3. Most importantly, we need to remember our connectedness to God.
    a. He made that connection possible and eternal, through Jesus Christ.
    b. The prayer medley is to help us reflect on that primary connection — our relationship to God through the priceless gift of his Son, our Savior, Jesus Christ.

Prayer Medley
"The Love Of God" (v. 1) F. M. Lehman
"I Cannot Tell" (vv. 1, 2) Londonderry Air
"Amazing Grace" (v. 1)
"Thank You, Lord" (chorus)

8 — Preparations For The Lord's Supper

Number 80

Litany

Pastor: Do you remember the story of the two travelers on the road to Emmaus?

People: They were sorrowing, confused, filled with both wonder and pain; for they heard that their Lord was alive; but they knew that he was dead.

Pastor: Then the Lord joined them on the road and walked with them and talked to them about the events of Easter. Yet, they did not recognize him.

People: That's remarkable! They look at him with their eyes, they hear him with their ears, and yet they do not see; they do not hear.

Pastor: Could that happen to folks today? Could it happen that the resurrection has happened for us, and we still do not grasp that fact?

People: We must admit that there have been times in our lives when the risen Lord has come to us, and our eyes were closed by self-concern and sinful motives.

Pastor: It was not until Jesus took the bread, blessed it, broke it, and gave it to them, that their eyes were opened and they recognized him.

People: Though they did not realize who he was, they sensed a presence they could not identify. "Were not our hearts burning within us while he was talking to us on the road!" they cried. *(Luke 24:32 NRSV)*

Pastor: Then, as we gather at the table of the Lord, we come with the prayer that as the bread is broken, our eyes also will be opened to the presence of the Lord. As we receive the cup, we too yearn to feel the burning in our hearts as we walk with the Lord, and receive from him the gift of life.

People: We celebrate the great good news, that that same Jesus who died on the cross, is alive, and "He's in the world today!"

Hymn: "He Lives" Alfred Ackley

Distribute The Elements Of The Lord's Supper

Number 81

Devotional Thoughts In Preparation For Receiving The Elements Of The Lord's Supper:

1. Supposing you were in the Sahel in Africa, surrounded by starving people.
    a. You have enough food for yourself to continue living and working in the region, but not enough to share with others.
    b. Would you be willing to refuse to eat the food yourself, while others around you were starving, and thereby, starve to death with them?
2. Supposing you were in a Southeast Asian nation where a terrible disease was passing through, fatal to everyone who contracted it.
    a. Something like the Black Plague in Europe.
    b. You have a vial for one shot of vaccine which will save you, while the others die.
    c. Would you be willing to give that vial to another and not protect yourself, so that you would die with the others around you?
3. Read Matthew 26:50-54
4. At his arrest and trial, Jesus refused the food and vaccine.
    a. He chose to perish with those who were perishing.
    b. Thousands of angels could have come to his aid, but he would not summon them.
    c. For only as he joined us in death could we join him in life.
5. The issue was self-surrender for Jesus. As we come to the table of the Lord, the issue is the same for us.

Distribute The Elements Of The Lord's Supper

9 — Reflections

1 — Definitions

Who defines your life? A parent? Your friends? What society says of you? The corporation? God? Whoever defines your life determines your identity, tells you what makes you a success or failure, and determines upon what conditions you have value. Many people spend their whole lives trying to live up to, or down to, the definitions that others have set for them. The problem is that any organization or person who can grant us control can also withdraw it out of spite, or to control, or because we no longer serve a useful purpose. Since we can't define our lives in isolation, it is imperative that we guard whom we allow to grant us worth, through their definitions. Most importantly, God defines our lives and gives us value beyond price. Through his definitions, we find our greatest freedom.

2 — Choices

Compared to my miniature poodle, I'm a giant. But size doesn't bother him, as he delights in romping with me on the floor. We go back and forth, wrestling and playing. As long as I don't trap his hind legs, he's free to get in or out of the game as much as he wants to. And he keeps coming back for more. Only when I trap those back legs and hinder his freedom, does he try to get away and stay away. In the Garden of Eden, God made an important decision — not to trap our hind legs. He gave us the freedom to get in or out according to our own choices. Only in that way could we freely love. In like manner, we must not trap the hind legs of those from whom we seek devotion. For in seeking to rob them of their freedom to get out, we deny them the freedom to choose love's yearning to get in.

3 — Germination

A couple of weeks ago, I re-seeded a portion of my lawn. As I raked the newly sown areas, some seed remained on top in the airy lightness of day. Other seed tumbled into the darkness under the dirt and peat which I raked back and forth. It is the seed which sank into the darkness of the soil that has germinated, while the seed which remained in the light of day is wasting away. It's in the darkest and loneliest moments of waiting and wondering, deep in the soil of pain, half fearful and half hopeful, that God plants his seeds of new life that germinate and take root. Here in a world without light, new prospects start to grow and new possibilities are given birth. As much as we yearn for the cheery light of day, it's in the dark soils of life where the richest and most fruitful events of living take root and grow.

4 — Time

Are you guilty of murder? Most of us are , at least to the extent that we are guilty of killing time. There's a difference between resting and killing time. All of us need to rest, to do nothing, from time to time. But killing time has to do with an attitude of investing ourselves in useless enterprises or the boredom of waiting around, until something better comes along. We only live for an average of 75 Christmases, or 3,900 weeks. Each week wasted can never be reclaimed; while each week invested in creative rest or constructive activity, builds foundations for meaningful and rewarding weeks and years yet to come. The Bible says, "there is a ... time for every matter under heaven." (Ecclesiastes 3:1) If we kill that time, it's forever lost, and some important "matters" go unattended. Time is a precious gift, and should not be the victim of a homicide.

5 — Building Arks

Build your ark while the ground is dry; for when the floods come, it will be too late to start looking for your hammer and saw. That's a rule of life that we seldom heed. When crisis and significant stress come to each of us, we normally have not planned in advance, particularly when it has to do with matters of the spirit. So we wait until we're in the Intensive Care Unit, or our marriage is coming unglued, or our child has spaced off into another world on drugs, before we look for spiritual resources to help us through our agony. That's something like waiting until the fire starts before going to the store to consider the merits of one fire extinguisher over another. If we find our peace with God during the good days, we'll already have our faith firmly in place when we need to draw from its well, in the day that trouble brings us to our knees.

6 — Natural Expressions

Jesus tells us the parable of The Good Samaritan, in which a foreigner stops to give aid to a brutalized robbery victim, after two religious leaders passed by, giving wide berth to any responsibility for this injured stranger. We most often focus on this story as an impetus to respond to social/racial issues. But Jesus told the story, not to stand alone, but to illustrate the primary issue under discussion: living in a loving relationship with God. (Luke 10:25ff) If that relationship is in place, as we respond with our whole beings, all other issues fall into place. We will respond to any need we see because we are threatened by no earthly barriers. The Good Samaritan story will be repeated in our lives, not because the story is a directive to us, but because it illustrates the natural expression of living in a loving relationship with God.

7 — Headlines

The tabloid headlines at the checkout stands are intriguing. Some stories are too grotesque to believe. Some are true, but are badly wrenched out of context, leaving a false impression. But if you stop to think about it, were you to remove typical headline grabbers like "shocking," "startling," "secret," or "scandalous," many of the items being addressed are rather normal life activities. People deceive one another, break each other's hearts, or struggle unsuccessfully with temptations that afflict us all. We usually like to laugh at, ridicule, or delight in, the pains of celebrities — which of course, is what sells those tabloids. Since we have to stand in line anyway, why not use the time constructively, not to ridicule, but to pray for those souls who are in trouble, that they might experience God's healing and blessing?

8 — Judgment

In our pluralistic society, we're told not to judge one another. We say, "My God is not your God; my moral values are not yours. You have no right to judge my moral activities by your value system." And yet, we cannot live in community, even as spiritual pluralists, without making judgments about one another's social and moral activities and either restraining them, or responding with help. The bigger problem with judgment than that activity itself is that we often link judgment with angry censure. Creative judging is done with a broken heart rather than with anger. It acknowledges the damage that sin has done to the sinner, even as it seeks to redress the injury done to others. The father yearned for the prodigal's return with a broken heart, not with anger. So, though judgment was required, restoration was assured.

9 — Being

The image comes to me of a man who looks small on a barren desert which looms large. He shakes his fist at the sky and cries out, "I didn't ask for this life!" And, of course, he didn't. None of us asked for the lives we have — where we were born, our sex, our race, our time in history. So the question of being was never our choice; but the question of what we do with our being is our choice. Long ago, a shepherd, David, did stand on the desert, stared at the magnificent sky, felt a kinship with the eternal presence, asked what is the value of being human, and discovered the priceless answer: "Thou hast made him a little less than God, and hast crowned him with glory and honor." (Psalm 8:5 RSV) With that certain knowledge of our priceless "beingness" in place, we are set free to find rich, new meaning in those things we do, whatever the context of our being might fashion for us.

10 — Easy Answers

It is so frustrating! "Just tell me the answer! Don't keep saying, 'Well, it depends!' " The car's not running smoothly? "Just fix it!" My emotions are out of control? "Just give me a sure-fire way to find peace!" "I haven't got all day! Just tell me God's will for my life!" Trouble is, concerning the important issues of life, there are no easy answers. There certainly are no simple answers. After all, human beings are not simple constructions. We can't be repaired like a lawnmower, or reassembled like a pre-fab bookcase. To suppose that there are easy answers to life's vexations and derailed goals is to deny our humanity. The very fact that we must struggle with complex issues and intertwining dilemmas is a verification of what marvelous beings we are. For we are created in the very spiritual image of God himself, who is the ultimate complexity of love, justice, and intricacy.

11 — Empowerment

The big dog is unperturbed by the incessant yapping of the small dog. The big dog knows he's powerful, and doesn't need to prove his superiority over the small one. The law of nature is that those who are truly powerful don't need to demonstrate that power. It should follow that as humans get more powerful, they need be less belligerent. Yet, reality shows that the more weapons we acquire, the more aggressive we normally become. The truth is, humans are not powerful by nature. Ours is a fragile power that's always under threat; thus the paradox: it's the most powerful and influential who are the hardest to deal with. The strength that allows us to be vulnerable, the power that allows us to be accessible, the inner resources which allow us to walk with a quiet dignity, is the empowerment that comes from God and brings with it security and peace, within the context of his will.

12 — Plight

Our plight is our task. Take away our plight, and we have no "raison d'etre." Often, like the apostle Paul, we cry out, "Lord, take this thorn from my flesh, then I can serve you well. Consider how much better I'd be able to function. Recognize what a witness I could be for you, were I healed." We cry out, "If I just had more money, a better education, improved health, a different career, a more understanding family, then I'd really shine. I'd make a difference in this world." But God's response to Paul was, "I'll leave you in your plight; for with that thorn, you will be far more effective than without it. We'll use it together to achieve victory." Our plights are part of our life experiences which give us the context in which we live our lives and find the fulfillment. Thus, in our plight, we find our reason for existence.

13 — Loneliness

In part, Easter is the story of victory over loneliness, and Jesus is the central figure in that drama. At his deepest agony in the garden, his friends abandoned him in sleep. At his trial, supporters and close, personal friends alike, couldn't wait to distance themselves from him. On the cross, even God seemed to have left him to his mockers and executioners. The soul separated from other lives and life, is the sound of the silent scream of spiritual pain. But Jesus moved through that tunnel of isolation to emerge from the tomb of death and loneliness, and assure us of fellowship and belonging to a God who loves his children beyond the grave. With the assurance that God loves us, we can risk letting ourselves be loved by those whose presence enriches, but now, whose absence does not devastate.

14 — Mixed Signals

Talk about split personalities! I saw a van last week that had a bumper sticker on the left side that said, "Hugs not drugs," and on the right side, a bumper sticker that said, "Happiness is seeing your boss' picture on the back of a milk carton." Love and affirmation on the left side, hostility and gleeful separation on the right side of the same van. That driver's mixed signals are typical of most of us who express love and indifference, vengeance and yearning for acceptance, in the same breath. Not only do we live with confusion in our souls, but we leave others who are dependent upon us, off balance, as they try to interpret who we really are and where we really stand. One of Jesus' goals was to lead each of us to a totally integrated life spiritually, physically, and mentally — a life of dependable goodness which is expressed in our every action and motive.

15 — Environmental Concerns

Many church kitchens have a sign that says: "Please leave this kitchen cleaner than you found it." The suggestion is that we not only clean up our own mess, but that we go a little further and delight other lives by making the area even better for our having been there. We might do well to carry that thought over to the human spirit. When we come into contact with others, they should leave our presence feeling better, more hopeful, relaxed and more upbeat than before our paths crossed. But that's a tough assignment; because, sinners that we are, we so often seem to want to get a couple of zingers in, or seek to make others feel as badly as we feel, or criticize another's performance in order to improve our own ratings. It's a sad thing when our goal in life seems to be to give a piece of our minds, rather than a peace of mind.

16 — Kites

Many who feel emancipated are merely disorganized. Freedom is a hard thing to handle, and as often as not, gets us into greater trouble than we had before. The only advantage is that it's trouble of our choosing, rather than that of another's choosing. We become like the kite that tugs against its twine in an effort to be free, but once loosed from its encumbrance, tumbles out of control, until it smashes itself on tree limb or rain gutter. The kite soars to the clouds, dips toward the earth and climbs again to new heights, precisely because of the perfect tension between the winds of freedom and the restraints of moral and religious conviction. In this connectedness, we're not in unbuttoned disarray, but in guided freedom, liberated from injurious restraints, using the tension of our lead to gain the heights of fulfillment.

17 — Mystery

The fun thing about a mystery is that it gives us a chance to solve a problem with an unknown answer. When we can't solve it, our frustration levels rise. In life, it's so important for us to have working answers that we'd rather live with false "certainties" than with operative uncertainties that are closer to the truth. So, if no rational explanation can be found for the untimely death, ill health, or devastating loneliness, then we say, "It's God's will," or "I must be so sinful I deserve this." There's less pain in this false certainty than in accepting the unanswerable as a part of life. Yet, if we'll let the buoyancy of faith in a loving God transport us over the unsolved mystery, we'll discover that his faithfulness is more supportive and important to our life's securities and satisfactions, than possessing the solution to the problem.

18 — Compassion

Variations on the phrase, "cast the first stone," come from Jesus' challenge to a hostile mob that wanted Jesus to condemn a woman to death by stoning, since she had just been caught in the act of adultery. He did not say, "Let he who has never committed adultery, cast the first stone." He did say, "Let he who is without sin, cast the first stone." (John 8:6) Frankly, we prefer to be barred from "executing justice" only when we've committed the same sin. That leaves us free to "fling at will," when we observe others falling where we are not vulnerable. But we have no cause to feel smugly self-righteous when we're strong at the point where others are weak. For those others are strong where we are weak. Jesus' point is that we are all in the "soup" together; and compassion is a far more appropriate initial response to sin than judgment.

19 — Helpers

The biblical story of human creation is rich with meaning and symbolism. When the newly formed woman is called a "helper," that comes from the Hebrew word that's used to refer to God as Savior, as when the psalmist says, "God is a very present 'Help' in time of trouble." (30:10) The symbol then, is that the female is created to "save" the male from aloneness: "It is not good that the man should be alone." (Genesis 2:18) Men and women save each other from aloneness. Bone of each other's bone, flesh of each other's flesh, we are at once different and the same, and created in a manner that requires relationship. When we live with pain in our souls, typically males and females seek to require subservience of the opposite sex. When we live as God intended in creation, female and male, we are interdependent sources of loving comfort and security for one another.

20 — Generations

I'm in one of those transition states — "passages" as one author calls it. AARP tells me I'm eligible for their "club." Cashiers are beginning to ask me about my senior citizen discount (for which I'm not yet eligible). When I was a child, I remember someone asking my 63-year-old grandfather if he'd like to be young again. "No," he said; life was fine for him, right where he was. I thought he had surely lost his senses. Who would choose to continue being old if he had the opportunity to be young again. Now I understand him. Our generation is who we are. We are a gift to it; it is a gift to us. Our identity, goals and ways of interpreting life are wrapped up in our generation. And we're all right, whatever slot we occupy in the passage of time. Every generation is special. Bishop Polycarp said it for all of us back in A.D. 155: "My God, in what a generation you've caused me to live!"

21 — Burglars

What angers me more than losing keepsakes when my home is burglarized, is to know that my space is not really safe. I can no longer leave my doors and windows open to freely come and go — even to cool off on a hot summer's night. Friends cannot run in without first gaining entrance through secured barriers. The thief robs me not just of things, but of a sense of openness to life. In like manner, when someone invites us into his inner life, and we carelessly or maliciously do damage to her soul with belittling remarks or humiliating accusations, violating the trust he has placed in us by inviting us into his inner sanctum, we become burglars, depriving that person of the privilege of vulnerability and the pleasure of an open door to life. The thief of inner and outer safety is at least as ravaging as the stealer of things.

22 — Down Time

There's no doubt about it. I'm one of those enlisted in the multitudinous ranks of the "Type A" personality. My agenda is overcrowded; my elasticity is at the outer bounds where strands could break. So I'm sympathetic with the frustration of those who must be sidelined for a time. But when we get beyond the anxiety of many things being left undone, there comes the revelation that down time can be a gift. Being sidelined is a time to embrace that which can never be achieved while being busy with an overburdened agenda. It's a time to taste discouragement, rest, test the pain, examine the ceiling — meditate, drift, connect. Down time is an occasion to receive rather than give, and to provide to others the gift of contributing to our needs. Finally, it's a time of rebuilding, repairing the body, and freshening the soul.

23 — Mailboxes

There are few things in our daily lives that bring greater positive anticipation than the mailbox. And there are few things that evoke greater disappointment than that same box when it's empty. We look forward to each day's mail in the hope that someone, somewhere, will think enough of us to send a message. If we get desperate enough for attention, even the computer letters that say, "You have been specially selected . . ." begin to look good to us. It's an important part of living to know that someone cares enough to take time to write and share some of the moments of their life with us. There is also One who wants to visit with us daily, and he's at your door right now. Jesus says, "Behold, I stand at the door and knock; if anyone hears my voice and opens the door, I will come in to him and eat with him, and he with me." (Revelation 3:20)

24 — Cupped Hands

Have you ever told someone something that's important to you; and all the while the listener observes you with a polite indifference on his unyielding face? It's like offering a prized possession to another, placing it in the palm of his hand; and he doesn't bother to cup his fingers over the present. The gift lies there, unclaimed, or rolls off the flattened palm. The bestower of the gift is more injured than if he'd been chased off without a hearing. To be politely heard, but not caringly considered, estranges us from the one whose interest or affection we seek. We err in our thinking if we believe that such civil courtesy accommodates any positive relationship. Children have been permanently turned away from a loving bond to a parent by such means. And many have missed glorious gifts of redemption and empowerment by being polite to God's entreaties to our souls.

140

25 — Reactors

I'm intrigued by the old saw, "I don't go to church as an adult because my folks made me go as a child." The same logic follows: "I don't read as an adult, I don't eat, or brush my teeth, or say 'thank you,' as an adult, because my folks made me do those things as a child." First, the argument makes no sense. But if it did make sense, it'd only indicate that we're as equally controlled by our contrariness now as we were by our parents' authority then and therefore, in neither case are we truly free. Liberation comes, not from stubbornly refusing to do something earlier forced upon us, but rather in gaining the freedom to do, or not to do, without it being a reaction. We miss many experiences that could be blessings in life because, in the name of freedom, we allow ourselves to be captive to reactive, negative emotions.

26 — Alarms

Someone said, "Cheryl knows her roast is ready when the kitchen smoke alarm goes off." There are some of us who never will get our lives perfectly together. Alarms go off continually, at work and home and school, telling us that the roast is done, or time's up, or the people are waiting. We presume that an organized mind is a gift of God — at least I hope so, since I fall into that category. But the Cheryls of this world are also gifts to us. For their "burnt roasts" remind us that life can't always be as neatly packaged as we'd like and we need to relax and regularly relearn that lesson. Beyond that, in spite of our harried lives, the Cheryls often feel rhythms, hear melodies, and discover marvelous oddities about life that we, whose roasts are cooked to perfection, miss, in the midst of our wonderfully organized agendas.

27 — Today

I'm a spring person rather than a fall person because spring has the beauty of today coupled with the promise of the coming summer delights. Fall has a beauty that can only promise the coming of cold fog and winter's drizzle. So for me, I can't fully appreciate today's colors because of my apprehension of tomorrow's cold. Admitting that makes me realize that I'm robbing myself of the blessings of today because of my anticipation of something that has not yet come tomorrow. Those who suffer ongoing pain, or the prospect of an early death, can teach us about enjoying the moment and letting today stand on its own, whatever may come, or not come, tomorrow. The Bible says, "This is the day the Lord has made, we'll rejoice and be glad in it." (Psalm 118:24) When we celebrate the gift of this moment, the good or evil potentials of the future become irrelevant.

28 — Safe Places

In some situations, I ask people with whom I am counseling, where their "safe place" was when they were children. It might have been a bedroom, a play house, somewhere in the woods, or near a mountain stream. People without a "safe place" are people in trouble. That "place" provides us with feelings of safety and intimacy with our surroundings. It's that place to which we always return when we need to pray, to reflect upon the great issues of our lives, or to draw strength from the quietness, solitude, and dependability of the surroundings. Jesus' "place" was the Garden of Gethsemane, and the home of Martha and Mary. This Rabbi, who had "nowhere to lay his head," nevertheless had his "safe places." Jesus needed them; so do we. Not only must we provide them for ourselves, we must carefully respect and protect those places for our loved ones, as well.

29 — Shopping Carts

Many of us come before God in prayer like we go through the supermarket with our shopping carts. Sometimes we carefully prepare a shopping list, and we pull only those items off the shelf to take to the checkout stand. Other times we impulse shop, and we take things off the shelf that attract the eye at the moment. We come before the Lord with our filled baskets, wanting him to accept our items, whether selected carefully or upon impulse. It's best for us to reverse the process and to approach God with our shopping carts empty, so that we may place the items in our baskets that are most helpful to us: insight into the real problem, healing for bruised psyches, encouragement for discouraged souls, hope for the hopeless, empowerment for those with a vision. Then we'll be sure to get those things which bring fruitfulness, joy, and fulfillment.

30 — Cables

In Washington State, the old timers remember the Starbuck ferry which transported cars across the Snake River. What caused me to marvel about this primitive craft was that it went from dock to dock, carrying up to six autos, and it had no engine. It was connected to a cable and the pilot propelled it from one side to the other by using the push of the current against the restraint of the cable, somewhat the way a sailboat tacks into the wind. Logs and debris float helplessly in the stream's current, but the ferry uses the force of the river to achieve its destination which, apart from the cable, would send it spinning out of control. The stream is the world. The cable is God's rule for life. Connected to the cable, we can withstand the heaviest stresses life can produce, using that potentially harmful energy to achieve our goal.

31 — Trees

A scourge of the emerging generations is their state of dis-connectedness. Partly it comes because we move so often. Part-ly it comes because we've learned to have no long term loyalty to any group. Partly it comes because we grow up in multiple families that separate and re-form, separate and re-form again in another configuration. In the process, we're robbed of both past and future. We must be like trees for life and growth. We must, at whatever age, have roots in the past, where we find our identity and center of belonging. We must also reach for the sky with our branches; for the sky is the future and the "new" which comes to us each day. Our nourishment for continued living comes both from the nutrients in the soil of the past, and from the elements found in the air of the future. And God is the continuity through it all.

32 — Hospital Gowns

One of the worst things about being a patient in the hospi-tal is having to take off our clothes, which define who we are, and put on those demeaning little gowns. Besides the fact that our bare fannies are flying in the breeze, there are certain items of dress to which we attach our dignity and identity. To one it's a wig and lipstick, to another it's the right shoes or a cer-tain style of jacket or slacks. We can salvage some dignity with an attractive robe or bed jacket. But in every case, forcing us into traditional hospital garb takes from us power, position, and self-image. Stripped of our props, each of us has to ask, "Who am I, apart from my uniform?" Actually, that's an im-portant question for each of us to address from time to time. It helps us redefine our purpose, our goals, and our personal value.

33 — Hope

For some of us, there comes a time when we lose hope. The world has gone dark, and there is no promise of light on the horizon. A wife or husband feels trapped by a spouse who's never going to change. Parents are caught by children that can never leave home to live on their own. My job is obsolete and I don't have the will or the opportunity to retain and relocate. "There's no hope! I've lost my future!" We must change the scope of our problems. None of us can handle forever. But most of us can cope with today, or at least, this afternoon. Since we can't know the future, we can't really know that it's hopeless. That being the case, we can let the future go and concentrate only on the hopelessness of the moment. And that in itself can give new reason to have hope, for that is something we can more easily manage.

34 — Valuables

Things possess the qualities of fun, value, or interest that we assign them. They have no intrinsic worth of their own. Gold, for example, is valuable only because human beings decide it is valuable. Keepsakes have value only because of memories connected to them by human minds. A name brand that's valuable today is worthless tomorrow because of our fickle feelings about fashion. The measure of what is valuable in life is not a measure of the thing itself, but a measure of the values of humanity. A good measure for discovering your own spiritual state of being is to examine what you count as valuable, and why. The worth you assign to various items and guidelines that you possess, or hope to possess, is an excellent measure of your spiritual health. Make certain your valuables will support you for eternity.

I remember in the 1950s, seeing Jackie Gleason run off stage near the end of his variety show, slip and fall, and break his leg. They cut away to a commercial, but the show had to be concluded without him. That's how it was in the early days of live television. Today, nearly everything is taped, and all bloopers and errors are edited out so that we see only a perfect program, perfectly produced. The trouble is, we begin to expect real life, and the daily actions of others, to be perfectly programmed with all errors edited out. But when we don't allow for the accidents and goofs in life, we're living in a fantasy world. One promise of the gospel is that as with the apostle Peter, so Jesus accepts us with our bloopers in place, and then gently leads us toward a perfecting life that only the Holy Spirit can work within us. *Going on to Perfection — but not there yet!*

36 — Self-limitations

"It's my life!" "This is my body!" We're very possessive of ourselves. We belong to no one else. Period! But it's not quite so simple as that. We didn't create ourselves so we have some obligation there. The Bible tells us that, in loving bonds, the husband's body belongs to his wife, and the wife's body belongs to her husband. (1 Corinthians 7:3ff) And again we read that our bodies are God's temples, (1 Corinthians 3:16) which implies a responsibility to a being outside ourselves. "You mean I don't have a life of my own?" No, that's not it. But it's too simplistic to claim that our bodies and lives are totally without involuntary interconnections. To claim that is not to grant us our humanity, but rather, to rob us of human qualities, which included self-limitation in order that other lives might be enhanced, along with our own.

37 — Journeys

There's a big risk in granting freedom to others. It becomes a burden to those who give it. Once others have received freedom, they'll make choices that present inconveniences to the grantors, or even threats to the power, position, and order of those ceding control. This is true of dictators who grant their people democratic reforms, and parents who give their children the right to make their own choices. Granting the right to choose not only permits strength and talent to come to the surface, but weakness and oddities to flourish, also. It gives rise to everything that produces friction and conflict, but there's no other route to the joy of seeing others find full humanity. For success, every step of this journey must be undergirded with prayer for a holy guidance and divine nurturing that we could never provide, even if we were in control.

38 — Just

"Just" is such a horrid little word. We use it most often as a put down of ourselves. "I'm just a housewife;" "I'm just a plumber;" "I'm just a woman," "I'm just a salesman or teacher;" "I'm just one man." It's demeaning when we refer to our personhood or our life's activities in that way. Some even use it to pray, saying, "I just want to thank you (praise you, ask you to do this for me)." The word refers to barely or very little, when used as an adverb in the latter example, or as a descriptive adjective, in the former. Regardless of our occupations, we are marvelously created beings. You're not just a person; you're a person, created in God's image, the supreme handiwork of the Creator. The psalmist exclaimed in amazement of man: "Thou has made him little less than God, and dost crown him with glory and honor." (Psalm 8:5)

39 — Gifts

The story of Job doesn't work for many of us who have known suffering because for Job, however badly it hurt, however much he lost in wealth and family, in the end, his fortunes were restored 200 percent. For most of us who suffer, that which we've lost is never restored. That's why the story of Job isn't found in the New Testament. Jesus never promises restoration and those who live with expectations that suffering is a form of dues paid that obligate God to a handsome payoff, are destined for disillusionment. Jesus doesn't explain suffering, but he uses it. The test becomes a testimony. What we've lost is not likely to be restored. But there's something new that can be discovered that's of equal, or of greater, value that we may gain. It's not a payoff earned through pain; it's a rich gift that becomes evident only in the crucible of life's fire.

40 — Loopholes

Loopholes are highly desirable in everything from income taxes, to real estate options to moral pronouncements. We seem wired to either invent, or search for, ways to reduce the size of the liability of our covenant or commitment. "Never give more collateral than necessary," is a self-serving rule that always leaves us on the edge, separated from the complete joy that could be ours with total commitment. This is particularly true in spiritual matters. A sweatshirt slogan asks, "How much can I get away with and still go to heaven?" Put up as little spiritual collateral as possible to secure heaven, while investing in earthly fun. Sadly, when that's our position, we diminish that which we "can get away with," with a guilty conscience, and rob ourselves of the fullness of spiritual joys that could be ours to enjoy here, and in eternity.

41 — Temptation

A prayer that's often in our heart of hearts, if not in our public utterances is, "O God, save me from the consequences of evil, but not from the pleasures of indulgence." If we call up the courage to be truthful about our inner feelings, it's not so often our desire to be quit of our temptations, which we really do find attractive, but rather, to be freed from the consequences of caving in to those temptations. These consequences include guilt feelings and self-recriminations, damaged relationships with those whom we love, or loss of opportunity to accomplish higher goals because of our destructive choices toward sin. We will not begin to have victory over our temptations and their consequences until we are prepared to search for greater pleasures in goodness, than we currently find in indulgence.

42 — Bonsai Christians

Bonsai trees are formed by stunting normal trees through a process of tying off the taproot so that the tree is forced to live off its surface roots. Stunted trees make attractive pieces for miniature gardens, but they have no value in providing lumber, shelter against storms, or homes for birds. Except for the fashion of it, they're useless. We make bonsai people, spiritually and morally, when we tie off the taproots that nourish their lives. We can do this to spouses or children, even to employees. It's tragic to see moral and spiritual dwarves who've never attained the stature for which they were destined, and who are living room ornaments instead of giants in the forest, because their taproots were never allowed to expand enough to draw sustenance and strength from the wellsprings of life through an intimate relationship with God.

43 — Disconnected

A person with amnesia has no past. And having no past, she has no meaningful present. And without a meaningful present, she has no hope-filled future. The Bible says that God came to the people of old, reminding them of their past before he tells them what he wants in the present: "I am the God of your fathers, of Abraham, Isaac, and Jacob . . ." In the New Testament, people feared that Jesus wanted to cut them off from their past by throwing out the law. "I've come, not to abolish the Law, but to fulfill the Law," he said. He did not intend to disconnect them from their heritage. We need that historical connection to give meaning to our present and future. When we cut ourselves off from our Creator, we develop a self-induced, spiritual amnesia that leaves us floating free of certain obligations; but also, it disconnects us from ultimate meaning.

44 — Ruts

There's a Canadian sign at a rural crossroads: "Be careful which rut you get into. You'll be in it for the next 20 miles." Being in a rut has negative connotations. But the flip side of the rut can be a football game with no goal lines, or a basketball game with no boundaries. If we have no parameters to our lives we find ourselves going about in circles with no ability to win or accomplish or conclude our journey. As the old saw puts it: "It is so soon I am done for, I wonder what I was begun for." Methuselah lived 960 years and died. In that near millennia he did nothing important enough to remember except that he lived, fathered some kids, and then died. Ruts that lead us to worthy goals have a number of advantages, including parameters that guide us to the prize of life. As each new stage of your life begins, consider carefully your goals and resolutions, and choose your rut carefully.

45 — Secrets

We must have secrets in order to be individuals and to be empowered. To share information, or to withhold it, is an essential right that every person deserves. In the old communist societies, a primary way of gaining control over people was to rob the citizens of their secrets. In pressing their children too hard, parents cannot only extract information that doesn't need to be known, but damage the integrity of the child, in the process. For spouses, friends, or parents to press to know everything there is to know about us is to rob us of the ability to manage our own lives and fail to admit that we are unique individuals who do not deserve to be overwhelmed by others, even when we're very small, and others are very big. Conversely, it's vital that we honor and protect the gift of a secret shared with us when someone trusts us that much.

46 — Healthy Grief

A widow came to the pastor at the close of the funeral service and asked, "When will I get over this?" He asked, "Do you really want to?" "No," she decided, she really did not want to. There's a fine line between inordinate grieving beyond healthy bounds, and retaining a cubicle of sweet sadness in a house that's filled with life. When we lose a child or a parent, a mate or a dear friend, if the love is rich, the pain of that love being broken is exquisite and to deny the poignancy of that severed relationship is to deny the love that it represents. On our own it's hard to find a good balance between healthy grief and warm memories. Rather than praying that God will remove all the pain, we might want to ask that he help us to maintain a sweet affection for that former bond fashioned in love, as we reclaim a healthy anticipation of the future.

151

47 — Grace

There's a popular slang phrase that begs another to ease up the pressure: "Cut me some slack," we say. Or, in reference to another upon whom we take pity, we plead, "Cut her some slack." We're asking that we not be held so tightly accountable by another. If we're in training to achieve a goal, then being held to a regimen by a coach or friend is necessary and worthwhile. But often, when we're holding someone else to stringent performances in daily life, we're really trying to work out through another, something we can't accomplish in our own lives. That's unfair. Thomas a' Kempis stated it beautifully in *The Imitation Of Christ:* "Be not angry that you cannot make others as you wish them to be, since you cannot make yourself as you wish to be." (Thomas a' Kempis, *The Imitation Of Christ,* Henneberry Co., Chicago, n.d., p. 14) We must grant others at least as much grace as God grants us.

48 — Commitment

"Make me feel good, Lord," is the prayer of some who seek an emotional high to counteract the daily downers of life. "Make it logical," is the Spockian demand of others who require of the Lord a neat, rational world that excludes surprises and mysteries. Neither approach is fulfilling; neither demand can satisfy our long term needs. Jesus tells us that we have to love God with all of our heart, soul, mind, and strength. Answers that are just emotional are too shallow; responses that are just spiritual, without relevant connections to daily life, are inadequate; commitments that are just intellectual are too restrictive, just as solutions which are physically combative can never provide the whole answer. An effective relationship with God that provides lasting answers requires the commitment of our whole being to his wholistic call.

49 — "They"

"They" is an ugly word. It robs us of our most precious gift — individualism. People who are the wrong age, speak with the wrong accent, have the wrong color of skin, work at the wrong job (or have no job), are all "they" to others. "Well, they are all like that, you know!" is an expression of damaging condescension. Being lumped into that sad category robs us of feelings, ideas, and recognition of our life's contributions. A precious treasure that we can grant any person who lives in a different group than our own is to hear his story, and recognize that unique contribution that he makes to our lives together. Today, I hope you have the opportunity to grant someone that special gift of individuality. It's exciting to discover that one of "them" has a name and a valuable idea to share.

50 — Joint Responsibility

One of the saddest of human experiences is divorce and often, those who suffer most are the children who are caught in the crossfire and impending cleavage. More than one million children go through that agony each year. One counselor pointed out that as parents and judges talk about the children, they should not talk about joint custody; rather, they should talk about joint responsibility. People are not things to be possessed. Instead, they are priceless, free beings, created in God's image to be loved, nurtured, and invited to participate in life to its fullest. The parents' emphasis upon finding ways to respond to the child's needs and healing his injuries, rather than demanding or rejecting custody of this possession, is crucial to the mental and spiritual health of children who need to be loved rather than to be kept.

51 — Elevators

The "3-Ds" that terrify us the most are disease, deterioration, and death. Suddenly our lives are out of control. We're sliding down the slippery slope, and there's nothing to grab onto that will hold us permanently without further decline. Sometimes panic or despair, at least resignation, start to take over. The apostle Paul suggests that for those who seek it, there's a different way to look at the "3-Ds." In 2 Corinthians 5, he suggests that our inevitable decline is the way to celebration and glory. It's something like the elevator principle. At one end of the cable is a huge weight. At the other end is the passenger car. As the weight falls downward, the car is lifted upward. In the same way, as our physical bodies deteriorate downward, our spiritual selves are lifted upward to the throne of grace.

52 — The Visitor

In yarns about visitors from outer space, alien life from the galaxy comes with power and sophistication that's greater than our own. The visitors arrive with a presence, force, and knowledge that's superior to ours, and control our responses with enough power to remind us that they're in charge. In contrast, God comes to earth without power, expressing himself through a vulnerable newborn baby. Sophistication is in short supply in the donkey stall of an overcrowded Bethlehem inn. Rather than bringing with him the full protection and resources of a spaceship, Jesus became one with us, accepted our limitations, and risked our acceptance or rejection. Without condescending to us from superior strength, he demonstrated that real power and ultimate victory come from the inner space of the spirit. That's an important part of the Christmas message.

Reflections Index